GW00371988

HOUSE OF LORDS

European Union Committee

17th Report of Session 2004-05

Proposed EU Integrated Action Programme for Life-long Learning

Volume 1: Report

Ordered to be printed 5 April 2005 and published 14 April 2005

Published by the Authority of the House of Lords

London: The Stationery Office Limited
£14.50

HL Paper 104-I

The European Union Committee

The European Union Committee is appointed by the House of Lords "to consider European Union documents and other matters relating to the European Union". The Committee has seven Sub-Committees which are:

Economic and Financial Affairs, and International Trade (Sub-Committee A)
Internal Market (Sub-Committee B)
Foreign Affairs, Defence and Development Policy (Sub-Committee C)
Agriculture and Environment (Sub-Committee D)
Law and Institutions (Sub-Committee E)
Home Affairs (Sub-Committee F)
Social and Consumer Affairs (Sub-Committee G)

Our Membership

The Members of the European Union Committee are:

Lord Blackwell	Lord Neill of Bladen
Lord Bowness	Lord Radice
Lord Dubs	Lord Renton of Mount Harry
Lord Geddes	Lord Scott of Foscote
Lord Grenfell (Chairman)	Lord Shutt of Greetland
Lord Hannay of Chiswick	Baroness Thomas of Walliswood
Lord Harrison	Lord Tomlinson
Baroness Maddock	Lord Woolmer of Leeds
Lord Marlesford	Lord Wright of Richmond

Information about the Committee

The reports and evidence of the Committee are published by and available from The Stationery Office. For information freely available on the web, our homepage is:

http://www.parliament.uk/parliamentary committees/lords eu select committee.cfm

There you will find many of our publications, along with press notices, details of membership and forthcoming meetings, and other information about the ongoing work of the Committee and its Sub-Committees, each of which has its own homepage.

General Information

General information about the House of Lords and its Committees, including guidance to witnesses, details of current inquiries and forthcoming meetings is on the internet at
http://www.parliament.uk/about lords/about lords.cfm

Contacts for the European Union Committee

Contact details for individual Sub-Committees are given on the website.

General correspondence should be addressed to the Clerk of the European Union Committee, Committee Office, House of Lords, London, SW1A OPW
The telephone number for general enquiries is 020 7219 5791.
The Committee's email address is euclords@parliament.uk

CONTENTS

NOTE:

The Report of the Committee is published in Volume 1, HL Paper No. 104-1.
The Evidence of the Committee is published in Volume 2, HL Paper No. 104-2.

References in the text of the report are as follows:
(Q) refers to a question in oral evidence
(p) refers to a page of written evidence

ABSTRACT

The current six-year EU-funded education and training programmes expire at the end of 2006 and the European Commission proposes to replace them with an ambitious revised programme, to run until 2013, costing three and a half times as much as the current programmes. These new proposals are set in the context of the Lisbon Summit goal of making the EU the world's most competitive knowledge-based economy.

The Commission proposes to expand present well-known programmes like *Erasmus*, for higher education exchanges, and lesser-known ones for schools, vocational training and adult education. A new underpinning programme would make sure that policy development, language-learning and ICT are better co-ordinated. Bureaucracy, which has bedevilled the present programme, would be simplified.

We find the present programmes valuable, despite bureaucratic drawbacks, and generally support the Commission's aim to improve and expand them. The new programme is in line with the Lisbon objective. But we doubt whether all the ambitious targets are attainable, how well they will cater for older and disadvantaged learners and whether the new administrative arrangements will be flexible enough. Better monitoring of the outcomes of the programmes is essential.

We urge the British Government to draw up and publicise a clear national strategy for making the most of these programmes and to tackle declining British participation in them. This would assist the beleaguered enthusiasts upon whom so much of the success of these programmes has depended in the past.

The Government should also consider the reasons why the United Kingdom is no longer the first destination of choice for foreign Erasmus students and tackle the serious lack of foreign language capability in this country. We also want to see British business more involved in planning the United Kingdom strategy and exploiting the opportunities offered by the new programme.

Proposed European Union Integrated Action Programme for Life-long Learning

CHAPTER 1: INTRODUCTION

Why did we carry out this Inquiry?

1. This Inquiry examines a Proposal by the European Commission (the Commission) to incorporate and build on the Commission's present education and training programmes by introducing a new comprehensive integrated life-long learning programme covering the period from 2007 to 2013.

2. It has been carried out by Sub-Committee G of the European Union Select Committee which deals with social policy and consumer affairs.

3. We decided to hold this Inquiry because:

   • the Proposal seemed at first sight to be far-reaching, politically important, ambitious and potentially expensive;

   • it was framed in the context of the goal set by the European Council at Lisbon in 2000 for the EU to become the most competitive and dynamic knowledge-based economy in the World by 2010;

   • it was also aligned with the Bologna Declaration in 1999 to create a "European area of Higher Education" by 2010;

   • we wanted to find out whether the Commission's present education and training programmes were well-conceived and relevant to the Community's needs, how well they worked in practice and what lessons might be learned from them in assessing the new proposals;

   • we also hoped to find out whether the proposed new programme was coherent, soundly-devised, with appropriate priorities, and likely to work well in practice;

   • since education remains essentially a matter for national competence within the EU, we wanted to be sure that the proposals fully respected the competence of Member States and the principle of subsidiarity;

   • we also wanted to know whether the proposed more than three-fold increase in the budget for the new programme was justifiable and offered the prospect of good value for money; and,

   • we were concerned that the needs of the programme should be given due priority when the Government judged the merits of the proposed budget in the context of overall United Kingdom policy on the new EU Financial Perspective.[1]

4. We were aware that the Commission's education and training programmes were last examined by the EU Select Committee in a Report on *Student Mobility in the European Community* in 1998.[2]

5. Some of the EU's present education and training programmes (notably the *Erasmus* programme for higher level education and advanced training) are quite well-known. But much less is known outside educational circles about others. We hope this Inquiry will focus attention in Parliament and more widely on what the Commission is doing and what they propose to do next.

6. We also wanted to find out whether the United Kingdom was making the best use of the opportunities presented by these programmes and to see whether more might be done to make better use of those opportunities in future.

7. In the shorter term, we also hoped that the Inquiry would help the Government's negotiations with the Commission and Member States over the new programme well before final decisions are required by the European Council and the European Parliament, and especially during the forthcoming United Kingdom Presidency of the EU.

8. For that reason, we have carried out this Inquiry rapidly and produced this Report as quickly as possible as a summary of our findings to date. In doing so, we recognise that more still needs to be done to examine this Proposal thoroughly.

9. We will continue to follow developments closely over the coming months when we anticipate that revised versions of the Proposal will emerge for fresh Parliamentary scrutiny before the new programme is due to start on 1 January 2007.

Conduct of the Inquiry

10. A list of the Members of Sub-Committee G who carried out this Inquiry and their declared interests is at Appendix 1.

11. The Call for Evidence was issued on 5 November 2004, inviting written evidence to be submitted by 10 January 2005. A copy is at Appendix 2.

12. Altogether we received 55 submissions of written evidence. We held seven oral evidence sessions, beginning on 19 January 2005 and ending on 2 March 2005. A full list of those that gave evidence to the Inquiry is set out in Appendix 3.

13. The written and oral evidence received by the Inquiry is printed in an Annex to this Report. We would like to express our thanks to all those who gave evidence to the Inquiry or assisted us in other ways while it was being carried out.

14. A glossary of educational acronyms used in the evidence given to this Inquiry is at Appendix 4.

---

[1] The negotiations on the new Financial Perspective are expected to be concluded during the forthcoming UK Presidency of the EU in the second half of this year and will determine the next EU budget for the period from 2007 to 2013.

[2] HL Paper 116, Session 1997-1998, 27th Report

Specialist Advisers

15. The Specialist Advisers to this Inquiry were:

- Professor Karen Evans, Professor of Lifelong Learning and Head of the School of Lifelong Education and International Development at the Institute of Education of the University of London, and

- Mr Mike Bourke, an educational consultant and former Chief Executive and Principal of Waltham Forest College.

We are most grateful to them for the contribution they have made to this Inquiry.

CHAPTER 2: BACKGROUND

The Commission's Present Education and Training Programmes

16. European Community activity in education and training started in the 1970s, based on articles 149 and 150 of the Treaty establishing the European Community (the Treaty). This activity was expanded during the 1980s and early 1990s into 6 separate programmes.[3]

17. Rationalisation took place in 1995 to create 3 programmes: *Socrates, Leonardo da Vinci* and *Youth for Europe*. The first phase of these programmes ran from 1995–1999. They were renewed to run from 2000–2006, and have undergone thorough evaluation by the Commission.

Socrates

18. The stated aims of the *Socrates* programme are:

- to strengthen the European dimension of education at all levels;

- to improve knowledge of European languages;

- to promote cooperation and mobility in education;

- to encourage innovation in education; and

- to promote equal opportunities in all sectors of education.

19. The *Socrates* programme is open to all EU Member States, the three EFTA countries (Norway, Iceland and Liechtenstein) and Bulgaria, Romania and Turkey.

20. The total budget for the present multi-annual EU budget for *Socrates*, which runs from 2000 to 2006, is €1.85 billion.

21. *Socrates* is divided into five separate programmes, mostly named after European thinkers. Each targets a different level of education. Box 1 shows the five separate divisions of the present *Socrates* programme.

BOX 1

Present Socrates Programmes

Comenius: to promote exchanges between schools and teacher training establishments and encourage the exchange of best teaching practice between countries to stimulate the learning of languages and intercultural awareness;

Erasmus: to promote transnational cooperation between universities to encourage European understanding and student mobility;

Grundtvig: to enhance life-long learning through transnational projects that range from a mobile educational unit to inform elderly people of EU policies to further education models for teachers at adult education colleges;

Lingua: to concentrate on ways in which language teaching can be encouraged and improved; and

Minerva: to promote European cooperation in the field of Information and Communication Technology and Open and Distance learning.

---

[3]   Erasmus, Comett, Lingua, Petra, Force and Eurotecnet

Leonardo da Vinci

22. The **Leonardo da Vinci** programme (*Leonardo*) has a separate budget of €1.4 billion for the present 7 year programme (2000–2006).

23. It aims to promote transnational projects based on cooperation between training bodies, vocational schools, universities, businesses and chambers of commerce to prepare EU citizens better for the labour market. The fund also provides grants for people to have a work-related stay abroad.

Tempus

24. **Tempus** is an additional higher education cooperation programme between the EU Member States and third countries bordering the EU and countries in Central Asia, North Africa and the Middle East. The scheme encourages 'Joint European Projects' between Member State universities and other universities with a clear set of objectives.

Erasmus Mundus

25. The **Erasmus Mundus** programme is a development of the *Erasmus* programme. It provides for cooperation and mobility in higher education to promote the EU as a centre of excellence in learning around the world.

26. It seeks to enhance the visibility and attractiveness in third countries of European higher education. It also provides EU-funded scholarships for third country nationals participating in Masters courses, as well as scholarships for EU-nationals studying in third countries.

Jean Monnet

27. **Jean Monnet** is a separate Commission project which aims to facilitate the introduction of studies related to European integration in universities by providing start-up subsidies. The project targets subjects in which EU developments are particularly important such as EU law, EU integration and political histories. It pays for academic teaching posts (Jean Monnet chairs), permanent courses in European studies and European teaching modules.

National Agencies

28. Each participating country has its own national agency which administers the main programmes. In the United Kingdom the British Council administers *Socrates*, except for *Erasmus*, which is administered by the United Kingdom Socrates-Erasmus Council based at the University of Kent, and pilot schemes, which are run by a commercial agency called ECOTEC.

Integration

29. A key issue at the time of renewal of these programmes in 1999/2000 was how to link and integrate them. Changes introduced included joint initiatives going beyond the scope of a single programme, as an interim step towards programme integration.

How well have the programmes worked in practice?

30. In 2002, the Commission launched an extensive public consultation to inform the development of the new phase of the programme due to start in

2007. The consultation showed that the programmes were generally regarded as both relevant and important, but the need for improved integration of the programmes was a central concern.[4]

31.   In March 2004 the Commission produced detailed interim reviews of the implementation of second phase of the *Socrates* and *Leonardo* programmes for the period 2000-2003[5]. This exercise included external evaluations carried out by independent consultants.

Socrates Programme Review

32.   The Commission's interim review identified "areas of progress" and "persistent difficulties". For *Erasmus* students undertaking study periods abroad, the review claimed real gains in cultural understanding, language competence and employability. But "persistent difficulties" included:

- financial barriers to the involvement of students from poorer socio-economic backgrounds;

- imbalances between countries, with candidate countries sending out many more students than are received while the United Kingdom and Ireland received many more than they could send;

- obstacles to teacher mobility, particularly in schools; and,

- over-complicated administrative procedures.

33.   The wider *Socrates* programme was shown to be widely regarded as successful at a European level in encouraging and supporting European awareness and cooperation through trans-national projects (where institutions cooperate to develop, for example, joint courses or teaching innovations).[6]

Leonardo Programme Review

34.   The review indicated several improvements since the first phase:

- decentralised administration to national authorities was considered to be an improvement;

- specific objectives were reduced in number, when compared with the first phase; and,

- overall, a positive view was taken on the first half of the second stage of the programme.

35.   "Persistent difficulties" included:

- objectives not matched by indicators, and therefore difficult to measure;

- complex administration;

- marketing and communication of programmes by the Commission and national agencies needing further improvement; and,

---

4   Commission documents 11587/04 COM (2004) 474 final and 11587/04 ADD 1 SEC (2004) 97 final

5   Commission documents 7211/04 COM (2004) 153 final and 7210/04 COM (2004) 152 final

6   Commission document 7211/04 COM (2204) 153 final, also summarised in Commission Documents 11587/04 COM (2004) 474 final and 11587/04 ADD 1 SEC (2004) 971, 15 July 2004).

- dissemination needing to be better-targeted, with more emphasis on developing best practice.

36. The independent external evaluation of *Leonardo* observed:

"the specific objectives are not quantified (no indicators); difficult to measure and that the general objectives seem too ambitious in relation to the means available. This makes the evaluations of the programme more difficult".[7]

---

[7] Commission document 7210/04 COM (2204) 152 final, also summarised in Commission Documents 11587/04 COM (2004) 474 final and 11587/04 ADD 1 SEC (2004) 971, 15 July 2004

CHAPTER 3: THE NEW PROPOSAL

37. On 15 July 2004 the European Commission published **A Proposal for a Decision of the European Parliament and of the Council establishing an integrated action programme in the field of lifelong learning.**[8]

38. As already noted in Chapter 1, this Proposal aimed to build on the Commission's present education and training programmes, which are due to expire at the end of 2006, by introducing a new comprehensive integrated life-long learning programme covering the period of the next EU Budget from 2007 to 2013.

39. The brand names and essential features of the best-known of the present programmes, including Socrates and Leonardo, have been incorporated in the new Proposal. As a result of the consultation, however, *Youth for Europe* was removed from the scope of the new Proposal on the grounds that it has distinctive features that would be eroded or lost through incorporation into the integrated Programme.

Lessons Learned

40. The current proposals have been drawn up with the primary purpose of achieving effective integration for the current *Socrates* and *Leonardo* programmes.

41. The Commission's review of the current programmes mentioned in the previous chapter had shown the need for further improvements in:

   - simplification of programmes, funding streams and administrative arrangements;

   - arrangements for devolution to national agencies;

   - reduction of barriers in access to programmes, both for individuals and organisations;

   - access to funding for activities and projects that are important but do not fit exactly into any one programme, and

   - assessment, coordination and dissemination of project outputs (including reduction of duplication and overlap).

Main Elements of the New Programme

42. Based on those evaluations, the draft decision proposes to replace the current programmes with four sectorally-defined programmes, integrated within a life-long learning framework.

43. The four sectoral programmes would be similar in scope to their predecessors and bear the same brand names, but have been re-defined as shown in Box 2.

---

[8]   Commission Documents 11587/04 COM (2004) 474 final and 11587/04 ADD 1 SEC (2004) 971

BOX 2

New sectoral programmes

Comenius for general education activities concerning schools up to upper secondary level;

Erasmus for higher education and advanced vocational education and training activities;

Leonardo for all other aspects of vocational education and training; and,

Grundtvig for adult education.

44. Activities in all four sectoral programmes would include mobility and exchanges for students, trainees, teachers and trainers, partnerships and "thematic networks" for exchange of best practice and multilateral projects for innovation and development.

45. A new *'Transversal'* **programme** would cut across the sectoral programme and would include:

- support for policy development in lifelong learning;

- provision of comparable data, statistics, research and analysis;

- promotion of language-learning;

- support for development of innovative ICT –based approaches; and,

- more substantial dissemination of results.

46. By incorporating language-learning and ICT in the *Transversal programme* the Commission intends to replace and develop the previous *Lingua* and *Minerva* programmes under a single administrative umbrella. The rationale is that language-learning and ICT development should run through all activities (in the jargon they will be "mainstreamed" rather than "bolted on").

47. A new *Jean Monnet* **programme** will also be absorbed into the Integrated Programme from 2009 to foster projects in European integration studies both within the EU and globally, through Jean Monnet chairs, teaching and fellowships, young researcher mobility and projects in the field of European integration. The programme already directly funds four European institutions[9]. Operating grants will also be available to support specific European institutions or associations active in education and training.

Policy Context

48. The Commission sets out the proposals in the context of the overall EU strategies shown in Box 3.

---

[9] The College of Europe (Bruges and Natolin), the European University Institute (Florence); The Academy of European Law (Trier); The European Institute of Public Administration (Maastricht).

BOX 3
Relevant EU strategies

Bologna 1999: established the 'Bologna process' to create a European area of higher education by 2010, signed by European Ministers of Education of 29 Countries

Lisbon 2000: Council set strategic goal of becoming the most competitive knowledge-based economy in the world, capable of growth and greater social cohesion

Goteborg 2001: Council agreed strategy for sustainable development and added an environmental dimension to Lisbon process

Barcelona 2002: Council set objective of making EU education and training systems a world quality reference by 2010; called for action to improve basic skills, including teaching of at least 2 foreign languages from an early age.

Copenhagen 2002: Council established process of enhanced European cooperation in vocational education and training. The Copenhagen declaration of Ministers of Education of 31 countries associated the social partners (unions/employers) and the 'candidate countries' to the process.

Key Commission Aims

49. The Integrated Programme has clear and ambitious targets:

   - 1 in 20 school pupils involved in *Comenius* activities during 2007-2013;

   - 3 million *Erasmus* students by 2011;

   - 150,000 *Leonardo* placements per year by 2013; and,

   - 25,000 *Grundtvig* "mobilities" (study visits) per year by 2013.

50. The Commission lays emphasis on the need for simpler and more flexible programmes, as recommended by public consultation and reactions from Member States and national agencies.

51. It says that administrative and accounting requirements should be proportional to the size of the grant concerned and administratively simplified. Derogations from existing Financial Regulations should be introduced where appropriate.

52. According to the Commission, the programme would not attempt to intervene in the structure or content of national education and training systems but would focus on areas where European added value can be engendered.

53. On proportionality, the Commission states that the proposal is designed to achieve the maximum simplification consistent with appropriate financial and procedural safeguards, in legislative definitions and in the administrative and financial requirements.

Funding

54. To fund this considerable expansion the Commission claims it will need a total budget of Euro 13.620 billion between 2007 and 2013. That represents an expansion of the present programme spending by more than 3.5 times.

55.   Minimum funding allocations to the sectoral programmes will be 40% to *Erasmus*, 25% to *Leonardo*, 10% to *Comenius*, 3% to *Grundtvig*. The remainder will go to the *Transversal programme* and other elements of the new programme.

56.   The proportion earmarked for *Erasmus* partly reflects the transfer of advanced (higher) vocational education and training from *Leonardo* to *Erasmus*.

Extended Impact Assessment

57.   The Commission's proposal is accompanied by a detailed Extended Impact Assessment (EIA)[10].

58.   This sets out aims for the potentially positive impact of the proposed integrated programme as follows:

- more extensive and better-quality co-operation between education and training systems and institutions throughout the Community;

- development of a European dimension in Community education and training, capitalising on trans-national comparison as an effective means of promoting change;

- improved quality of education and training systems and learning provision;

- increased volume and better quality of mobility of learners, teachers and trainers;

- improved innovation, economic competitiveness and entrepreneurial spirit;

- better adaptation of systems for social change and of work-forces to industrial change;

- improvement of transparency, recognition and portability of qualifications throughout the Community;

- improvement in language and ICT skills;

- enhanced equality between men and women and equal opportunities for the disabled and other disadvantaged persons;

- reduction in xenophobia and racism; and,

- enhanced knowledge and awareness of European integration issues by academics and the general populace.

59.   The EIA reports on the extensive stakeholder consultation carried out by the Commission. While generally positive about existing programmes, this highlights the need for: improved administrative and financial procedures (current ones being perceived as disproportionately burdensome and slow); more synergy and coherence between actions and programmes; better dissemination of good results and avoidance of excessive detail in the legislative design of programmes.

60.   Those consulted also felt that the *Youth Programme* should be kept entirely separate.

---

[10] 11587/04 COM (2004) 474 final ADD 1

British Government's Preliminary Views

61.   In an Explanatory Memorandum (EM) (pp 1-6) on the Commission's proposal dated 31 August 2004, the Department for Education and Skills says that the Government recognise that transnational co-operation can add value to education and training in Member States through the transfer of innovation, experience and best practice.

62.   The Government also acknowledge the importance of the programme's support of the Lisbon goals, including the contribution of life-long learning to social cohesion and the need for those who left education without basic qualifications to have a second chance to gain the education and training they need.

63.   The specific objectives proposed to promote creativity, competitiveness, employability and social cohesion are endorsed by the Government. The EM also welcomes the emphasis on greater de-centralisation and on enhancing language and ICT skills.

64.   But it sounds a warning note over the proposed increase in the budget. It says it will not be possible to agree the budget until the overarching negotiations on the new EU Financial Perspective have been concluded. But the Government will aim to ensure that the budget is "proportional to the European value added by the programme and is focussed on the most effective activities within the programme".

65.   The EM states that the Government aim to test the efficiency and added value of the Commission's proposals in negotiation and stresses the need for the sectoral programmes to be well co-ordinated and managed to ensure coherence and synergy.

66.   The Government will also strive to ensure that sufficient priority is given to vocational education and training and to improving employability, as well as better access to education for disadvantaged groups. They also want to see more effective and outcome-focused monitoring and evaluation of programmes and intend to seek clarification on how de-centralisation will work in practice.

CHAPTER 4: EXAMINING THE PROPOSAL: ROLE OF THE COMMISSION

Competence

67. Because education is essentially a matter of national competence[11], the Commission's policy has gradually evolved as described in Chapter 2.

68. Box 3 in Chapter 3 describes the series of Decisions and Declarations which form the policy context for the Commission's Proposal. We wanted to be sure that the Proposal was properly within Community competence and that the policy context on which it was based was sound.

69. The Commission pointed out that, although responsibility for education and training lay with Member States, the Treaty invited the EU to support Member States in delivering quality education and training through instruments such as interchange, exchange and mobility (Q 43).

70. The Government told us they believed that the Commission had a valuable role in helping Member States to improve the quality of education and training within their own national systems. It was consistent with the proposed Treaty base of Articles 149 and 150 (Q 2).

71. The British Council added that the Commission's role was necessary because it would give coherence and the necessary mechanism for cooperation between Member States. Without the intervention of the EU, the Council thought this co-operation would be less effective. (QQ 11 and 12). This view was supported by Universities United Kingdom (UUK) (Q 68) and by the University Association for Contemporary European Studies (UACES) (Q 128).

Subsidiarity

72. We asked several witnesses whether the Commission's role might be intrusive. None of them found it to be so. (Q 69, Q 128, Q142, Q 175). UUK said that they got the maximum benefit from the present programmes while encouraging minimum intrusion from the Commission (Q 69).

73. The Commission told us that Member States decided their own priorities within the programme and that the Commission did not wish to impose a straitjacket on them (Q 59).

74. Although their EM confirms that the Government is "satisfied with the Proposal on grounds of subsidiarity", it adds that "in negotiations the Government will seek to ensure that the language of the Decision is fully consistent with the principle of subsidiarity". (pp 1-6)

75. **We conclude that the Commission's role in relation to these programmes is an appropriate one, and carried out with due respect for national competence.**

---

[11] Under the EC Treaty the Commission can only encourage co-operation between Member States and support and supplement Member State action in educational matters. Responsibility for national education policies (including the content of teaching and the organisation of their education systems) remains with Member States.

76. **Nevertheless, we recommend that the Member States in Council should continue to ensure that the Commission's plans and actions in developing this Proposal are appropriate, proportionate and fully consistent with the principle of subsidiarity.**

Policy coherence

77. Of the various decisions and declarations cited by the Commission as the policy basis for the programme, we felt that the Lisbon and Bologna Declarations were the most important.

Lisbon

78. At a special meeting of the European Council in Lisbon in March 2000 the EU Heads of State and Government agreed on a 10 year strategy aimed at making the EU "the most competitive and dynamic knowledge-based economy in the world, capable of sustainable growth with more and better jobs and greater social cohesion" by 2010.

79. The EU Education Council was tasked to devise "concrete future objectives of education systems, focusing on common concerns and priorities while respecting national diversity"[12] As noted in paragraph 12 of Chapter 3, this led to subsequent Council decisions at Goteborg in 2001 and Barcelona and Copenhagen in 2002 which also contributed to the Commission's strategy for the programme.

80. A High Level Group, chaired by former Dutch Prime Minister Wim Kok was charged by the European Council to examine progress and make recommendations to give renewed impetus to the Lisbon process and to contribute to the Commission's mid-term review of the process. The Group's Report (the Kok Review) [13] called for inter-connected initiatives in the knowledge society, the internal market, the business climate, the labour market and environmental sustainability to keep the Lisbon process on track.

81. The Kok Review stressed the importance of attracting and keeping the best researchers, giving high priority to research and development, innovation and promoting information and communication technologies (ICT). It also called for strategies for life-long learning and active ageing. Although subsequent discussion of the Kok Review has tended to focus on competitiveness, the overall Lisbon goals remain a cornerstone of Community policy.

82. The Government told us that the proposed new programmes were "very much within the context of the Lisbon process… and all that that entails in terms of the skills of people who work in the EU". They said British Ministers were "looking for the programmes to support the Lisbon process" Doubts over whether the Lisbon targets would be met within the time set tended to make the proposed programme even more important. (Q 1).

83. UUK agreed that the programme proposals were clearly related to part of the Lisbon Strategy and would help the implementation of that strategy because they would contribute to employability.(Q 66) UACES concurred and

---

12 Quoted in Commission Document 11587/04 ADUC 144 SOC 365 CODDEC 924

13 *Facing the Challenge*: European Communities Official Publication Office 2004 ISBN 92-894-7054-2 (See also written evidence from the Work Foundation at G146)

confirmed that, in their view, the Commission's proposal was coherent (Q 128). Other witnesses agreed (pp 282-289 and pp 262-264).

84. Professor Roger Vickerman, Jean Monnet Professor of European Economics and Director of the Kent Centre for Europe, argued that increasing levels of ability and understanding between people of different Member States were a vital component of the Lisbon Agenda. Students needed to be adequately prepared for the future European labour market. (pp 292-294).

85. The Work Foundation (pp 300-301) saw education and skills as a decisive component in the Kok recommendations. A comprehensive life-long learning strategy was "an essential building block in the delivery of a higher quality labour market with highly trained and educated citizens more capable of not only realising their potential, but creating and enjoying the fruits of a knowledge economy".

86. But both the Government and UUK pointed out that, since it was not due to start until 2007, the proposed programme could only make a limited contribution to the achievement of the Lisbon goals by 2010. It had to be seen in the longer context. (Q 3, Q 66)

87. **We conclude that the proposed new Programme is broadly consistent with the Lisbon objective of making the EU a more competitive knowledge-based economy. It should make a positive contribution to that goal in the longer term. But, since the programme is not due to start until 2007, it cannot be expected to make much impact by 2010.**

88. **We recommend that the Programme should be seen as a long-term investment in building European capacity to prepare future generations for the challenges of globalisation and to enable the present working generation to improve and extend their skills.**

Bologna

89. The other key element in the Commission's policy is the so-called Bologna process. This is not a Commission initiative. It stems from a meeting of 29 European Ministers responsible for higher education in Bologna in June 1999. They agreed to lay the basis for establishing a European Higher Education Area by 2010 and for making the European Higher Education Area attractive to the rest of the World.

90. The process agreed at that meeting included: adopting a system of comprehensible degrees and higher education cycles; a common system of credits; promoting mobility by overcoming obstacles; fostering European cooperation in quality assurance; and the promotion of European dimensions in higher education. At subsequent inter-governmental meetings this process has been extended to some 40 participating countries.

91. The Government told us that, although the Bologna and Lisbon processes were different they regarded them as complementary and aimed at the same goals. Between them, the processes were setting a framework for open voluntary co-ordination between Member States in which the proposed life-long learning programme would play a significant part. (Q 2)

92. Again UUK and UACES agreed. By contributing to better opportunities for good employment, UUK thought that the Commission's proposals would help to give the Bologna process increased momentum (Q 66). UACES pointed to the common thread of promoting a European dimension among

participants and saw the Bologna process as building on the experience of the Commission's *Erasmus* programme (Q 128).

93. Written evidence from several respondents welcomed the Commission's linkage between the proposed programmes and Bologna (pp 270-271, pp 292-295 and pp 234-239). HEURO (the Association of United Kingdom Higher Education) stressed the important contribution to the Bologna objectives of mobility, which was a key feature of the proposed new programme. (pp 243- 256)

94. But, as with the Lisbon objective mentioned above, because the new programme is not due to start until 2007 it cannot be expected to make more than a limited contribution to the achievement of the Bologna goals by 2010.

95. **We conclude that, especially because of the emphasis on mobility, the proposed programme is broadly consistent with and should help to further the Bologna objectives. But it must be seen as a broad-based, long-term investment in life-long learning with a much wider range than higher education with which Bologna is concerned.**

96. **Nevertheless, between them the Lisbon and Bologna commitments do seem to us to represent a coherent and complementary policy framework for the proposed new programme.**

CHAPTER 5: EXAMINING THE PROPOSAL

Overall Shape and Approach of the Proposed New Programme

97. Without exception, those of our witnesses who are already involved in current EU education and training programmes broadly welcomed the new programme. They saw it as building soundly on programmes which they regard as essentially valuable and relevant. But they pointed to serious shortcomings over funding and bureaucracy, which had already been reflected to some extent in the Commission's mid-term review of the present programmes. It was evident that many of the witnesses also felt discouraged by the relative lack of attention, encouragement and support they received in carrying out these programmes.

98. The Commission defined the essential factors underlying the Proposal as:

   • increasing integration between education and training throughout Member States;

   • the challenges posed by demographic change, especially the need to sustain an ageing population for longer active working life and to meet changing occupational needs;

   • the demands of a more competitive society within and beyond Europe;

   • the need to build on the strengths of existing programmes and to tackle the shortcomings; and

   • the need to simplify and rationalise budgetary and administrative arrangements (Q 42).

99. Commission witnesses noted that European education and training was characterised by diversity, richness of innovation, and the capacity to generate different perspectives on similar problems. But innovation tended to be locked behind national barriers. It needed the stimulus of personal interchange. Member States should be encouraged and supported in learning from the experience of each other (QQ 42-43).

100. They also acknowledged that the programme also had a very clear underlying EU citizenship objective to engender greater participation and mutual understanding among Member States (Q 44).

101. The Government took the view that the overall shape and approach of the proposed programme seemed to be "going in the right direction" although with room for improvement on details. They welcomed the Commission's emphasis on simplification and felt that the Commission had consulted widely before framing the Proposal (Q 40).

102. They also stressed the importance of:

   • encouraging mobility, innovation and exchange of best practice;

   • ensuring clear objectives, effective management of processes, improved evaluation focusing on outcomes and better dissemination; and,

   • giving more emphasis on vocational training and adult learning and more attention to social inclusion (Q 1).

103. They acknowledged the contribution which the programme could make to the potential dynamism of the single European market (Q 8).

104. The Government, the British Council and the Commission all assured us that great importance was already attached to social inclusion in these programmes. But the Commission confirmed that they had not attempted to judge the success of the inclusivity of any of the programmes and that the onus lay mainly with national agencies to make sure that disadvantaged groups were properly catered for (QQ 37-38, QQ 56-58).

The Individual Programmes

105. Against that background, we will examine the evidence given about the Proposal, starting with the four main strands where, as already noted, the brand names and essential characteristics of the main current programmes have been retained. We will then examine the new features of the Proposal, including the administrative issues which the simplification proposals aim to address, and the increased funding proposed.

CHAPTER 6: ERASMUS

106. This is the best known and, in many ways, the flagship of the EU education and training programmes. It concentrates on higher education and is founded on long-standing traditions of European scholarship exchanges.

107. We had a great deal of supportive evidence from universities and representative bodies with considerable experience of the present *Erasmus* programme. Most wanted to see the programme expanded. But several questioned whether the target to increase overall student mobility participation in the programme to 3 million by 2011 was achievable (Q 24, Q 75, pp 262-264, pp 270-271, pp 223-225 and p 240).

108. The chart at Figure 1 shows the numbers of students taking part in *Erasmus* between 1995/96 to 2002/03 which tends to support the view that the proposed expansion is very ambitious and may be unattainable. The cumulative number of students taking part between 1998/99 and 2003/04 was only 691,567 which is far short of the proposed target of 3 million between 2007 and 2011.

FIGURE 1

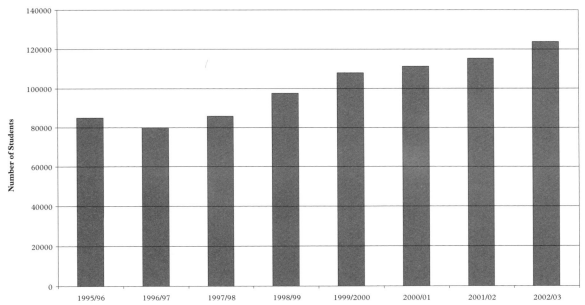

Total Number of Students Participating in Erasmus

109. UUK and UACES argued strongly that *Erasmus* grants to students and institutions must be significantly improved for the new programme to succeed. Inadequate provision for administration costs deterred many British universities from taking part (Q 65, Q 77, Q 102, Q 138, Q 141, pp 77-80 and pp 60-64). Several universities and HEURO agreed. (pp 262-264, pp 270-271, pp 258-262, pp 223-225, pp 218-219 and pp 243-256).

110. The United Kingdom Socrates-Erasmus Council acknowledged the concern of universities over the inadequacy of the provision for the costs of organising mobility and the grants for teacher mobility, but was less sure that student grants were inadequate (Q 172).

111. UUK, UACES and HEURO also argued that the proposed arrangements for funding were not sufficiently flexible. Grants should be available for shorter periods of study abroad. More and more students were taking part-time degree courses. The programme did not allow short-term mobility, which was particularly prejudicial to older students and those with work and family commitments. Short-term assignments and visits to more than one country could also provide valuable field work experience (QQ 70-71, Q 73, Q 81, Q 58-159, and pp 243-256).

112. UUK told us, quoting from a recent study by the Higher Education Funding Council for England (HEFCE)[14], that British Erasmus students were "predominantly young, white, female, middle-class with good European language skills". They argued that older students and part-time students, as well as those with insufficient or under-developed European language skills, those whose first language was not English, and those with family and work commitments would be more likely to be attracted to more flexible, tailor-made programmes covering shorter periods and with more realistic levels of support (pp 60-64).

113. They suggested that the increasing diversity of students in higher education in the United Kingdom was probably greater than that of comparable Continental European institutions. But this was not reflected by British *Erasmus* participants who were mainly concentrated in the 20-24 age group. Despite the commitment of universities to widen participation, only 7 per cent of students aged over 25 and only 2.5 per cent of students aged over 30 took part in *Erasmus*, whereas the current United Kingdom population of United Kingdom higher education students over the age of 30 was 8.9 per cent. (QQ 71-74).

114. UUK acknowledged that British universities should do more to link *Erasmus* participation with the widening participation initiatives they already under way. But they re-iterated that better resourcing and more flexible rules more closely tailored to the needs of older and part-time students and those with family responsibilities would help (QQ 115-118). UACES agreed (Q 133).

115. Several witnesses pointed out that current *Erasmus* funding arrangements assumed that similar numbers of students would be exchanged between participating countries. As a result, institutions were not eligible for support grants for students from other participating countries. This put British universities at a particular disadvantage since far more *Erasmus*-funded

---

14 International Student Mobility (HEFCE 2004), Report by the Sussex Centre for Migration Research and the Centre for Applied Population Research, University of Dundee, 'International Student Mobility' (July 2004).

students came to the United Kingdom from other participating countries than British students went abroad on *Erasmus* awards (QQ 102-104, QQ 136-137, pp 262-264, pp 292-294, pp 223-225 and pp 218-219).

116. We were concerned to learn that the number of British students taking part in *Erasmus* mobility programmes was declining while the number of outgoing *Erasmus* students from France, Germany and Spain was increasing (pp 90–97) . This is illustrated in the graphs Figures 2 and 3. We comment on the national implications in Chapter 16.

FIGURE 2

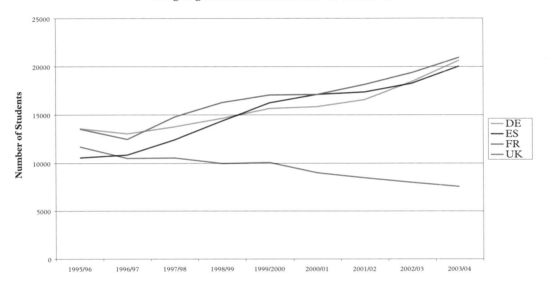

Outgoing Erasmus Students 1995-96 to 2003-04

FIGURE 3

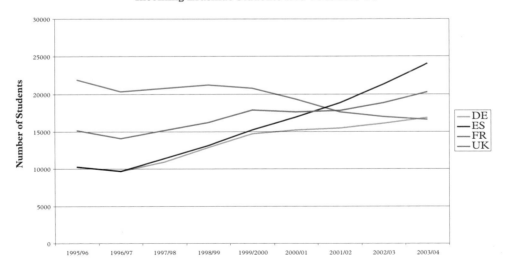

Incoming Erasmus Students 1995-96 to 2003-04

117. Several respondents praised the advantages to individual students and teachers from *Erasmus* programmes. Professor Vickerman added that *Erasmus* had also led to the development of new types of study programme which were integrating complementary activities in partner universities. He believed this was making a positive contribution to the Bologna process (pp 292-294).

118. The United Kingdom Socrates-Erasmus Council welcomed the proposal that students should be able to apply for more than one *Erasmus* grant (pp 90-97).

119. Several witnesses pointed to the need for *Erasmus* to allow more scope for post-graduate students (Q 89, Q 141, Q 158, and pp 265-267).

120. London Metropolitan University advocated more flexible links between *Erasmus* awards and EU-funded research fellowships (pp 262-264).

121. Several respondents claimed that the present European Credit Transfer System (ECTS) for common recognition and transfer of academic credits did not measure student workloads in a uniform way, as it was intended to do. They contended that this could put students at a disadvantage when carrying out *Erasmus*-funded study periods in other countries. It was undermining the effectiveness of the *Erasmus* programme and tending to deter students from taking part. (pp 282-289, pp 290-292, pp 223-225, pp 230-231, pp 90-97)

122. We have had some evidence about the proposal that the separate *Jean Monnet* project should be merged with the new Programme in 2009 and about ways in which the new *Jean Monnet* programme might be developed (pp 258-262, pp 292-294, pp 77-80). We note that this project is highly regarded by those respondents. But, in the time available and with the over-riding need to focus on the main programme proposals, we do not feel able at this stage to reach any conclusion or make any recommendation about that aspect. Nevertheless, we hope to be able to examine that proposal carefully when it is submitted for further Parliamentary scrutiny.

123. **We conclude that the priority given in the Proposal to the *Erasmus* programme is understandable and valid in principle. But we share the doubts expressed in evidence that the target to increase *Erasmus* student mobility to 3 million by 2011 is attainable.**

124. **We therefore recommend that the Commission should reassess that target and give serious consideration not only to the effect that the concentration on *Erasmus* may have on other programmes, but also on the need to ensure that students and institutions taking part in *Erasmus* are adequately funded and supported.**

125. **In doing so, we also recommend that the Commission should pay particular attention to the adequacy of the provision for the costs borne by institutions in organising *Erasmus* mobility.**

126. **We further recommend that the Commission should examine whether the present *Erasmus* programme is sufficiently inclusive and whether more ought to be done through extra funding or more flexible rules to provide for more short-term mobility and to tailor programmes in other ways more closely to the reasonable needs of older and part-time students and those with work or family responsibilities.**

127. **We note that the present funding arrangements for *Erasmus* are based on an apparent assumption that roughly equivalent numbers of students would be exchanged between participating countries, which is clearly disadvantageous to the United Kingdom and some other participating countries. We recommend that the Commission should reconsider the theoretical assumptions which have led to this practice and bring forward proposals for a more equitable basis for funding.**

128. **We also recommend that the Commission should consider making the rules more flexible to allow for more post-graduate *Erasmus* placements and links with EU-funded research programmes.**

129. **We note the concern that has been raised with us that inconsistencies in the present European Credit Transfer System (ECTS) tend to put students at a disadvantage when carrying out *Erasmus*-funded study periods in other participating countries and to deter students from taking part in *Erasmus*. We recommend that the Commission should investigate these claims and report to Council on whether they are well-founded and, if so, what should be done about it.**

CHAPTER 7: LEONARDO DA VINCI

130. The *Leonardo da Vinci (Leonardo)* programme focuses on vocational education and training from upper secondary school level through to continuing vocational education and training. It funds placements for trainees in enterprises or training institutions, professional development placements and exchanges for teachers and trainers, guidance counsellors and others responsible for vocational education and training (broadly known as mobility projects). It also funds pilot projects to improve training systems, develop networks of expertise, including language competencies and the production of reference material.

131. The new *Leonardo* programme aims to increase placements to at least 150,000 a year by the end of the Integrated Programme. Its focus on vocational education and training makes it particularly relevant to the Lisbon objectives.

132. Evidence from further education colleges and non-profit organisations involved in running *Leonardo* programmes was overwhelmingly positive about the benefits for the personal development and skills training of those taking part (Q 204, QQ 220-223, Q 287, Q 288, pp 278–279, pp 135–142, pp 132–135, pp 142–144, pp 122–125 and pp 121–122).

133. This was broadly supported by evidence from the City and Guilds of London Institute (pp 228–229). The Universities Council for the Education of Teachers (UCET) commented that the new *Leonardo* proposal would offer good quality professional development opportunities for tutors (pp 289–290).But, as with the *Erasmus* programme, several witnesses felt that the structure was not sufficiently flexible to meet the needs of older students and those with work or family responsibilities (Q 205, QQ 238–9, and pp 122–125).

134. Despite the problems involved, several witnesses spoke impressively about what they had done to devise successful programmes in areas with a high proportion of disadvantaged young people (QQ 256-257, Q 281, Q 307, pp 142-144 and pp 122-125) and to alleviate local structural unemployment (Q 294, pp 142-144).

135. We heard again about the inadequacy of management cost provision, especially for smaller colleges and not-for-profit organisations (Q 200, Q 231, Q 243, Q 248, Q 283, Q 296, pp 142–144, pp 122–125, and pp 243– 256). We were also told that the funding for travel costs was insufficient for those living in remoter areas (Q 298).

136. It was clear from this evidence how heavily the burden of bureaucracy fell on smaller organisations and how that could impinge on successful participation (QQ 225–228, Q 231, QQ 233–234, QQ 240–244). One witness told how participation in her college had had to be reduced because she was on maternity leave without a replacement (Q 229).

137. One witness gave a particularly interesting example in the way in which *Leonardo* partnerships have contributed not only to raising skills in United Kingdom forestry but also stimulated awareness of new products and processes that have been of tangible commercial value to British forestry businesses
(Q 282, QQ 287–88, and pp 135–142). (See Box 4)

BOX 4
Forest Recreation—Leonardo da Vinci

As the forestry sector in Europe undergoes great changes, diversification of forestry beyond timber to recreational and conservation use is creating a need for training, technical updating and development of skills. A training organisation (Grampus/Clark MacTavish) has been working to create a better match between training provision and modern forestry industry needs, exposing students to the wide range of innovative practices in Europe. This has involved mobility projects in 28 European countries with over 2,000 people travelling out from the United Kingdom through *Leonardo*, for periods between one week and 6 months. Grampus is currently leading a seven nation project for developing forest based recreation. Although examples can easily be transferred between countries, this often does not happen because common training and dissemination systems are not in place. Pilot projects have been set up to develop, produce and implement common modules of training to overcome these problems. Through these activities it has been possible to build up a very large network of partners, some of whom have become commercial partners for United Kingdom forestry organisations. Through *Leonardo* activities, Grampus has introduced some 10-15 new forestry skills to the United Kingdom, as well as products and processes developed in participating European countries that have been used in sustainable forestry management in the United Kingdom and even exported from the United Kingdom to third countries.

138. Another witness gave us details of Scottish conservation and heritage projects that had benefited from extensive *Leonardo* support (pp 132–135). (See Box 5)

BOX 5

Scottish Conservation and Heritage Projects—Leonardo da Vinci

In another *Leonardo* project 66 Scottish practitioners in areas of conservation, environmental management and forestry have been brought together with their counterparts in Finland, Germany, Slovakia, Iceland, Ireland, and Slovenia. The main objective was to promote reciprocal transfer and application of best practice and sustainable development in environmental management, and provided an opportunity for Scotland's managers to gain new skills and expand their international perspectives.

139. Colleges spoke of the difficulties of attracting support from the business sector (Q 235). But others demonstrated that through good local contacts and effective personal promotion commercial support could be secured (Q 292, Q295). The Welsh Assembly Government gave interesting examples of successful *Leonardo* projects involving businesses in the Principality (pp 295–299).

140. Witnesses also stressed the importance of:

- building successful partnership relationships;(Q 302)

- making the effort needed to find new partners in the newer participating countries (Q 302); and,

- effectively disseminating good practice amongst colleges and voluntary organisations (Q 195, QQ 197–98 and pp 105–108, pp 121–122).

141. Several witnesses welcomed the transfer of higher education work placements from *Leonardo* to *Erasmus* under the new Programme (pp 262–264, pp 77–80, and pp 60–64). The Institute of Electrical Engineers (IEE) stressed that vocational training should be carried out within a structured qualification and skills framework that was recognised by individuals, employers, professional bodies and training providers (pp 256–258).

142. The European employers organisation (UNICE) commented that the *Leonardo* programme evaluations were often available too late for project promoters and administrators to learn from them and called for a better monitoring system and more effective strategies for dissemination (pp 282–289).

143. Several witnesses said that the requirement to find match funding (i.e.: to secure contributions from other sources to the overall cost) for *Leonardo* placements placed an unreasonable burden on smaller, tightly-funded organisations and especially voluntary bodies (Q 197, pp 301–303, pp 267–269, pp 273–274). The Learning and Skills Council suggested that a co-financing approach, as used in ESF funding, might be more appropriate (Q 462, pp 178- 180) We are unable to comment on this, but it appears to deserve consideration by the Commission.

144. **We conclude that the *Leonardo* programme is of considerable potential significance for the Lisbon agenda and appears, from the evidence we have been given, to have achieved a great deal in some cases. But much seems to depend on the admirable commitment and ingenuity of dedicated individuals in small organisations who lack adequate support.**

145. **We recommend that the Commission should examine the rules for the *Leonardo* programme to ensure that they are sufficiently flexible to meet the needs of part-time and older students and those with family responsibilities, as well as disadvantaged groups and those living in remoter areas.**

146. **The Commission should also examine whether the funding levels for the administration of *Leonardo* projects are adequate, especially for smaller colleges and not-for-profit organisations, and consider what else might be done to support such organisations and make their task easier.**

147. **We also recommend that more consideration should be given by the Commission to improving ways of disseminating good practice and spreading awareness of the positive benefits, especially for employers, of taking part in the *Leonardo* programme.**

148. **We further recommend that the Commission should examine the suggestion made to us that the match-funding requirements of this programme place an unfair burden on smaller tightly-funded organisations, and especially voluntary bodies, and that they ought to be changed.**

CHAPTER 8: GRUNDTVIG[15]

149. Like *Leonardo*, the *Grundtvig* programme needs to be examined for the contribution it might make to the Lisbon agenda. With its focus on adult education, we saw also saw it as a challenge to the validity of the Commission's aim to create a genuine life-long learning programme.

150. We had much less direct evidence on *Grundtvig* than on *Leonardo*, which underscores our impression that it is a relatively neglected programme. But the National Institute of Adult Continuing Education (NIACE), whose members are heavily involved in the current United Kingdom *Grundtvig* programme, claimed that it had:

- given adult learners from different countries "a new and welcome experience" in working together;

- enabled numerous British adult learning organisations, large and small, to gain access to European programmes and valuable experience at working with European partners;

- encouraged innovation aimed especially at "hard to reach adults"; and

- yielded good value for money from relatively small amounts of funding (pp 108–111).

151. The following examples in Box 6 were produced by the Department for Education and Skills (pp 38–58) to illustrate how imaginative Grundtvig projects can cater for the needs of disadvantaged adult learners:

---

[15] Nikolai Frederik Severin Grundtvig (1783-1872) was a Danish clergyman and writer and is regarded as the founder of the Nordic tradition of lifelong learning. His "folk schools" were based on the idea that education should be available throughout life and should embrace citizenship and personal development. (Source: European Commission website)

BOX 6

Grundtvig Projects: Inclusion

HM Prison Maghaberry, Northern Ireland – MABEL (Multidisciplinary approach to adult basic education and learning)

Students, particularly those with basic skills deficiencies, were encouraged to participate in the writing and production of a magazine *Open Doors* in collaboration with students in prisons in Ireland, Norway, Bulgaria and Poland.

"We had contributions from students who have autistic problems and suffer from major problems in literacy and numeracy."

"The acquisition of basic skills, which is at the core of this project, complements and supports the United Kingdom government's key educational priority of developing and improving adult basic literacy and numeracy."

Ridge Danyers College, Stockport – *ALIA (Adult Learners in Arts)*

Artwork made by the students from Greece, the Netherlands, Bulgaria and Spain accompanied by introductions to highlights of national art history was posted on a web-based platform. Participants developed language, ICT and curating skills and deepened their knowledge of the cultural history of their own and partner countries. Staff have shared good practice in introducing learners from informal arts education to formal education.

"As a direct result of the project, the College intends to open a facility for blind and partially sighted learners. New software has been introduced and a training manual has been produced for mainstream trainers to better equip them with the skills needed to work with blind and partially sighted learners."

152. Our evidence indicates that many of the factors involved in planning and carrying out successful *Grundtvig* programmes are similar to those already identified for the *Leonardo* programme:

- the growth in part-time education and training and the personal commitments of older learners requiring more scope for shorter-term assignments (Q 205);

- the strong emphasis on the disadvantaged and social improvement (Q 37, Q 207 and pp 229–230); and,

- the problems caused by excessive bureaucracy and inadequate funding, especially for the smaller organisations which appear to be the driving force in this type of activity (Q 200).

153. College programme organisers stressed the need for careful preparation, good organisation and adequate debriefing if projects involving older learners were to succeed This tended to require a more intensive commitment of management time and effort than for some other programmes. (Q 204, Q 207, pp 267-269).

154. NIACE saw the need for improved integration between *Grundtvig* and *Leonardo* projects, including the possibility of developing joint projects and pooling funding streams (Q 198). UACES thought that the integration proposed under the new programme should lead the professional education

departments in universities to pay more attention to *Grundtvig* opportunities (Q 132).

155. Both the Third Age Trust and Help the Aged drew attention to demographic developments which, in their view, demanded more adequate and suitable training for older learners, whether to continue in paid employment or to make a valuable contribution to society through voluntary work. (pp 274–278, pp 242–243).

156. The Commission's new Green Paper on demographic change[16] reinforces the importance of focussing the *Grundtvig* programme on older learners. It states that by 2030 the number of older workers aged between 55 and 64 will have risen by 24 million compared with 2005. The number of people who are aged 65 and older will be 52 per cent or 40 million higher than today. Over the same period the number of people of what is traditionally regarded as working age is predicted to fall by 6.8 per cent or 20.8 million As a result, it is most likely that older people will need to continue to play some form of economic role in European societies.

157. We asked the Government to what extent *Grundtvig* was achieving the life-long learning objective. They replied that "in legal terms" the programmes were "age blind", but could not say how many over 60s, for example, were taking part in Grundtvig programmes (Q 22).

158. Much of the discussion in evidence turned on the proposed allocation of only 3 % of the new programme budget to *Grundtvig*. The Commission admitted that "at first sight" the proposed allocation of 3 % "seems rather shocking". It acknowledged that demographic trends added to the importance of improving European adult education (QQ 49–50). But it pointed out that the proposed budget catered mainly for less expensive short-term mobility and small-scale partnerships. It also drew attention to the constraints on the mobility of adult learners when compared with university students and the limited absorptive capacity of some of the sectors involved. Even so, the Commission thought that the target to increase individual adult mobility to 25,000 by the end of the programme was ambitious (Q 49).

159. UACES also considered that the allocation of 3% was not unreasonable when comparing the average time spent abroad of some seven months for the 3,000 students targeted under the new *Erasmus* programme with the average of a week or so for the 25,000 adult learners targeted under the new *Grundtvig* programme (Q 131). But UUK argued that the limitations on mobility faced by older learners ought not to be a reason for limiting *Grundtvig*. (Q 77). NIACE agreed. It believed that more than 3% was needed and questioned the Commission's assumptions about how much mobility might be managed. (Q 207, pp 108–111).

160. The Government told us that the proportions to be allocated to individual programmes had not yet been discussed between Member States and the Commission, pending negotiations on the new Financial Perspective. But they saw *Grundtvig* as a "very useful vehicle for building adult basic skills" which was currently oversubscribed in the United Kingdom and had produced good results (Q 20).

---

[16] Commission Green Paper "Confronting demographic change: a new solidarity between the generations" COM (2005) 94 final.

161. The Commission's rationale for the relatively low allocation proposed for *Grundtvig* seems to us to be based partly on a questionable circular argument about the relatively low previous take-up by older adults. Instead of citing the barriers that many older learners face as a justification for lower allocation, we believe the new programme should strive to overcome those barriers imaginatively and sensitively. Unless more flexible and innovative modes of training, aimed at overcoming barriers and allowing more adults to participate, are incorporated in the new programme it will fail to be truly life-long and inclusive and will not meet the challenge of demographic trends.

162. We asked about the relevance of ICT and distance-learning to *Grundtvig*. Witnesses responded that adult learners tended to need more encouragement and support when using ICT, but that ICT was increasingly being used effectively to enhance mobility projects and develop links between institutions and with individual learners. The use of broadband links for education institutions in the remoter parts of Scotland was a good example of what might be achieved elsewhere in Europe (QQ 210–11).

163. It seems to us that ICT and distance-learning systems based partly on ICT, as described in the written evidence of the Open University (p 270), would be ideally-suited to the needs of adult learners for whom the *Grundtvig* programme is intended. Well-designed and properly-supported distance-learning programmes should be able to prepare adult learners cost-effectively to make the most of the limited mobility their circumstances may be able to offer. It could also provide valuable continuing contacts and further training once mobility visits had been completed. In some cases, suitable distance-learning systems could help those who are unable to travel to keep pace with fellow students who have been able to travel. An attractive and sensitively-designed distance-learning package could also give older learners an added incentive to improve their computer skills.

164. **We conclude that the *Grundtvig* programme, like *Leonardo*, can make a significant contribution to the achievement of the Lisbon goals. But *Grundtvig* is also an acid test of the Commission's commitment to genuine life-long learning and, from the evidence we have been given, we are not convinced that the new *Grundtvig* programme is sufficiently well-tailored to the needs of older learners and the additional support they are likely to require.**

165. **We recommend that the Commission should give more consideration to demographic trends in Europe, as well as the inclusiveness and life-long learning aims of the overall programme. These factors suggest to us that more than the proposed 3% of the programme budget should be allocated to *Grundtvig* and we recommend that the Commission should re-examine the rationale for that allocation.**

166. **In framing the new packages for both *Leonardo* and *Grundtvig* we also recommend that the Commission should consider whether more innovative use of ICT and suitable distance-learning packages might help to overcome obstacles to participation, as well as encouraging improved computer capability for older participants.**

CHAPTER 9: COMENIUS[17]

167. This programme promotes exchanges between schools and teacher training establishments up to and including upper secondary level. It can fund:

- exchanges with schools in other participating countries through visits by pupils and teachers and other links;

- initial and in-service training and work experience for teachers in other participating countries;

- school development projects aimed at sharing experiences on teaching methods, school organisation and management and other themes of common interest between participating schools;

- other partnership and co-operation projects between participating schools;

- language projects, including the teaching and learning of less widely-used European languages; and,

- the development of subject-based information networks between schools[18].

168. A survey of 311 British teachers conducted in 2002 by the United Kingdom National Foundation for Educational Research (NFER)[19] that had taken part in *Comenius* school projects showed the benefits illustrated in Boxes 6 and 7.

BOX 7

Benefits of participation in Comenius

66% of those questioned said that participation in a Comenius project had increased pupils' willingness to learn other languages

Of the 836 projects in 2002, 490 included foreign languages as a curriculum theme

Other benefits reported by teachers in the same survey included:

Improved knowledge and skills: e.g. project management skills, improved subject knowledge, use of ICT in teaching, cross-curricular teaching methods;

Professional benefits from working with teachers in partner schools, observing classroom teaching in other countries and sharing practice, refreshed interest in teaching.

Impact on pupils: improved knowledge of countries and cultures, motivation to learn and active participation in learning activities

97 per cent said that they would recommend participating in Comenius projects to other schools and teachers.

---

[17] Born in what is today the Czech Republic, Joan Amos Comenius (1592-1670) was an educator who worked for peace and unity between nations. He was convinced that education was the only way to achieve full human potential. Source: European Commission website)

[18] Commission document 11587/04 COM (2004) 474 final

[19] David Sims (2002) NFER Survey Report: Comenius 1 School Partnerships, National Foundation for Educational Research.

BOX 8

Inclusion

Statistical evidence on 'approved applications from disadvantaged groups' provided by DfES/British Council indicates a reduction in approved applications as a percentage of total applications, as follows:

- schools in economically disadvantaged areas: approved applications 25% in 2001, 18% in 2002 and 12% in 2003; figures for 2004 not yet available .

- schools with substantial numbers of pupils at risk of exclusion: approved applications 18% in 2001, 17% in 2002, 14% in 2003

- schools with substantial numbers of pupils with special educational needs: approved applications fell from 12% in 2001 to 11% in 2002, 3% in 2003

A new category of "geographically disadvantaged areas" appears in the statistics for the first time in 2003, accounting for 6% of total applications.

169. Professor Robert Fisher of Brunel University, who has been involved with *Comenius* projects for more than ten years, submitted that the programme inspired pupils and teachers to forge creative partnerships with schools elsewhere in Europe. This added a valuable European dimension to the teaching and learning already taking place in those schools. It gave teachers and school managers the opportunity to share and develop professional knowledge and skills and broadened their international horizons. But he considered that more flexible funding would augment the opportunities for extra staff to visit schools taking part in the projects and that projects should be evaluated more rigorously (p 239).

170. The Welsh Assembly Government reported overwhelmingly positive responses from Welsh teachers and pupils involved in *Comenius* projects. Welsh teachers saw it as a useful tool for professional development which also enhanced their cultural awareness. It had increased children's motivation to learn other languages, acquire ICT skills, improve their literacy and take more pride in their work (pp 295–299).

171. Mobility was seen as an essential element in the value of *Comenius* for both teachers and pupils. Other developments, such as e-twinning of schools, added more value to the experience (pp 295–299). Two of our college witnesses spoke very positively of *Comenius* projects in which they had taken part for teacher-training, language development and school partnerships for those with learning difficulties(QQ 260–261).

172. To gain a better understanding of *Comenius* we arranged, with the help of the British Council, an oral evidence session for two educational advisers and the Heads or Deputy Heads of three schools—one primary, one secondary and one special needs school—who had considerable experience of *Comenius* (QQ 317-410). This illustrated very vividly how much can be gained from *Comenius* in broadening the horizons, enhancing the motivation and self-esteem, and stimulating the creative imagination of school children (QQ 375–382, pp 163–168, p 170, p169).

173. The teachers described how, with determination and ingenuity, mobility projects can be extended to disadvantaged pupils, including the disabled (QQ 385–389). They told us *Comenius* also made a very positive contribution

to the professional development of teachers and support staff (QQ 403–405, pp 163–168, p 169).

174. The main problems highlighted by the teachers were, once again, the inadequacy of the grants to cover costs (Q 388) and bureaucracy (Q389). They praised the importance of the support they received from the British Council (Q 406). Although some local education authorities were supportive, the overall picture was described as being inconsistent (Q 383).

175. This evidence was broadly supported by the two educational advisers. One worked directly for the City of Bristol LEA. The other, based at the International Resource Centre at the University of Hull, assisted schools in the Yorkshire and Humberside region (QQ 318–319).They spoke in similar terms of the value of *Comenius* (QQ 321-322, Q 326, p 153,) and about the burden of bureaucratic procedures on schools (QQ 367–369).

176. Both the advisers and the teachers drew attention to the need for more effective strategic guidance and encouragement from Government and LEAs to make the most of *Comenius* and promote it effectively to schools. They said this was one reason why only around 1 in 25 British schools took part in *Comenius* (QQ 333–341, QQ 391–396).

177. Both the advisers and the teachers also pointed out that in the United Kingdom, unlike in some other participating countries, the cost or unavailability of supply teachers to cover for the absence of teachers taking part in *Comenius* was a serious stumbling block (QQ 351–352, Q 402).

178. *Comenius* was seen by both the advisers and the teachers as improving ICT awareness. Although English was often the working language for school projects, teachers found that the interchange heightened language awareness and emphasised to pupils the importance of learning languages (Q 354, QQ 400–401).

179. The following example in Box 8 taken from written evidence (pp 163–168) from one of the Head Teachers who took part in the above-mentioned oral evidence session, demonstrates how much an imaginative Comenius project can achieve, even for small primary schools in a rural area:

BOX 9

Comenius

Benhall St Mary's and its partner schools Bosmere and Hardwick, all Suffolk primary schools, are coming to the end of a highly successful three year School Development Project, with partners from Belgium, Latvia and Lithuania. For several years now the three schools have participated in the Socrates Comenius 1 School Partnerships, funded by the European Commission and administered by the British Council.

How and why were they inspired?

The schools began with all the right ingredients for success. Suffolk has strong links with Flanders, partly through its connection with the Flemish Ryckevelde Foundation, a charitable organisation which promotes and supports European cooperation. This meant that there was a secure basis, from the start, for a highly organised educational partnership. Taking their school improvement plans, the project co-ordinators in each of the schools looked at how Comenius 1 could enhance these and raise pupils' achievement.

Improving pupils' thinking skills in order to raise achievement

This was an emphasis of all the cross-curricular projects but was a particular focus of an inspiring Art project. All the partners chose an artist of their country and the children "copied" a picture of that artist. They then went on to create a new picture in the style of the artist. Pupils found this extremely challenging because they had to solve a variety of problems. They used their sketch books as "thinking logs", identifying when they got stuck and how they got themselves "unstuck". Their approaches were compared and found to be similar in all the countries. In one of the Suffolk schools a creative partnership was established with the artist who wrote to the teachers advising them on types of paint and approaches. The outcomes were moderated by all partners and a high standard of work was recorded from all countries. All schools are continuing to challenge and develop pupils' thinking.

---

180. We were greatly impressed by the enthusiasm, dedication and ingenuity of the teachers active in *Comenius* projects who gave us evidence. They are an outstanding example of what can be achieved from these projects by pupils, school staff and the schools themselves. Their efforts deserve more recognition and, as we comment in Chapter 16, more needs to be done by the British Government and Local Education Authorities (LEAs) in this country to support them and encourage more British schools to follow that example.

181. **We conclude that *Comenius* is an important and imaginative programme with considerable potential which deserves more recognition and support.**

182. **We recommend that the Commission should look more closely at what needs to be done to encourage greater awareness and participation in *Comenius* and to remove unnecessary bureaucratic obstacles which impede effective participation and place unfair burdens on the dedicated organisers of these programmes, especially in smaller schools.**

CHAPTER 10: VALUE OF THE PRESENT PROGRAMMES

183. As will be evident from the preceding chapters, we have had abundant anecdotal evidence of the value of all the programmes described above. All the individuals and institutions taking part had consistent and broadly positive views, derived from that anecdotal evidence, about the wider value of the programmes. We also received a great deal of statistical material from the Commission, the Government and other sources.

184. This anecdotal evidence repeatedly emphasised the so-called "soft" benefits of participation such as character development, confidence-building and cultural awareness. Individual case histories illustrated qualifications gained, skills acquired and obstacles overcome, often admirably. The statistics told us a great deal about the volumes and trends in numerical terms. All in all, these produced a very positive picture reflecting great credit on the individuals and institutions involved.

185. But we were unable to find evidence of any systematic qualitative analysis of the benefits of the programmes, especially in the longer-term. We asked various witnesses about this.

186. Although the Government praised the Commission's interim evaluation reports on the *Socrates* and *Leonardo* programmes, they commented: "We would always like to have a little bit more focus on real outcomes rather than counting the bodies involved" (Q 40).

187. The Commission talked about the "overwhelming weight" of anecdotal evidence in favour of the programmes. This showed that they were clearly of great significance to the individuals involved and would collectively "translate into benefits for society and for the economy, even though it is difficult to measure them" (Q 40).

188. UUK accepted that not enough qualitative analysis had been carried out and that "a lot more outcome-based evaluations" were needed, both of existing and proposed programmes. But the rather limited qualitative analysis they had seen indicated "enormous benefits in terms of maturing... enhancing academic study and enhancing employability and people getting better jobs and enhancing promotion within that employability once they acquire it" (Q 83). UUK agreed that more systematic international evaluation of achievements would be welcome (Q 84).

189. On the other hand, the Director of the United Kingdom Socrates-Erasmus Council described Erasmus as "probably the most evaluated programme I've ever come across". He explained that the Council produced an annual report collating the evaluation reports from the students and teachers who took part in Erasmus as well as reports on student conferences. Studies were carried out by other bodies. But long-term evaluation was difficult because universities did not keep good alumni records. Member States should be encouraged to develop an Erasmus alumni database from which a "longitudinal study" could be extrapolated (Q 185).

190. NIACE were not aware of any official structured research on the benefits for adult students from mobility programmes. Attempts to secure funding for such research had failed. The Association of Colleges agreed (Q 203).

191. Witnesses from colleges taking part in the *Leonardo* and *Grundtvig* programmes thought that qualitative assessment would be difficult when so

many of the benefits for individuals were essentially subjective. But the benefits for institutions of pilot projects, for example in curriculum development, could be measured. They called for a national forum for dissemination of results (QQ 220-223).

192. Witnesses from non-profit organisations involved in *Leonardo* programmes pointed to tangible benefits for relatively small-scale businesses in the forestry sector and in managing wetland conservation schemes. But on the whole, small organisations could not afford the costs of systematic long-term evaluation (QQ 287-290).

193. Among other evidence, the European employers organisations UNICE advocated a monitoring system to identify good results from projects more rapidly and disseminate them more effectively (pp 282-289). SPRITO, a sports based education and training charity, called for "post-project outcome tracking" to assess the penetration and difference made by projects for up to 12 months following completion (pp 273–274).

194. **We conclude that the evidence we have been given, while anecdotal, amounts when taken together to a consistent, comprehensive and impressive picture of the value of these programmes. Despite some obvious shortcomings, the weight of evidence demonstrated to us significant improvement of individual skills, as well as character development, confidence-building and cultural awareness of those taking part. This should enhance the employability of individuals and contribute significantly to the overall European knowledge base, in-line with the Lisbon objectives.**

195. **We also conclude that participation in these programmes has enriched the lives of participants and contributed to the development of networks of useful cooperation between individuals and institutions in participating countries. Educational institutions in those countries have undoubtedly been strengthened, in-line with the Barcelona objectives.**

196. **We further conclude that the better understanding of the political, economic, commercial, historic and cultural significance of participating countries and European institutions which these programmes offer to those who take part in them, and the personal and institutional links that can be developed from them, should be of lasting value.**

197. **Nevertheless, we recommend that the Commission should consult with Member States and interested parties about the best way of devising a more systematic qualitative as well as quantitative analysis of the benefits and shortcomings of all the programmes for both the individuals and the institutions taking part, as well as for the wider benefits for the EU and other participating countries.**

198. **We further recommend that this analysis should be designed to inform future national strategies, as well as contributing to more effective dialogue between the Commission and participating countries about possible improvements whenever the programme is reviewed. But we believe it is essential that it should not add unduly to the bureaucratic burden on participants, especially from small organisations.**

199. **We also recommend that, having devised this system, the Commission should make sure that the results are widely disseminated in an easily-understandable format to Member State Governments, national agencies and both actual and potential participants in the programmes.**

CHAPTER 11: MAIN FEATURES OF THE NEW PROGRAMME: INTEGRATION

200. The three main new elements of the Programme are: Integration, the Transversal programme and simplification. The other is the greatly increased budget proposed.

201. The Commission states[20] that the integrated approach which gives rise to the title of the new programme is "designed on the one hand to preserve essential continuity with past experience... and on the other to increase the coherence and synergy between all its constituent parts".

202. This involves:

- transferring advanced vocational education from the Leonardo to the Erasmus programme;

- oversight of the whole programme by a single programme committee comprising the Commission and Member State representatives; and,

- the incorporation of the previously separate Jean Monnet project from 2009.

203. The Government told us that the creation of the single programme committee should improve cohesion because it should be able to take an overview of all the different strands of the programme. It should also help to speed up administrative decisions (Q 13).

204. The Commission claimed that this would lead to better integration between education and training, the distinction between which had been increasingly difficult to define. It would reinforce the strength of existing programmes whilst addressing "discontinuities and problems" (Q 42). Project deadlines would be harmonised and projects could be transferred from one programme to another (Q 43).

205. UUK considered that the proposed integrated structure should encourage coherent programme promotion and management and hoped it would also help to make the new systems more user-friendly for institutions (Q 65). UACES also saw the integration of the four strands as very positive. It should encourage closer cooperation between universities, schools and adult education institutions. Funding levels, budget procedures and application deadlines, which were currently all different, should be harmonised and simplified (Q 132).

206. The Association of Colleges also welcomed the creation of a single programme committee and the introduction of common actions and procedures under the Transversal programme. It hoped this would enable joint projects to be carried out by blending funding streams so that a genuinely joined-up approach could be achieved (Q 196, Q 198).

207. Other evidence also welcomed the incorporation of higher education vocational training in the Erasmus programme and the formation of a single programme committee in the hope that it would lead to genuine streamlining (pp 282–289, pp 262–264, pp 265–267).

---

20 11857/04 COM 2004 474 final

208. **We conclude that the proposals to transfer vocational training at the higher education level from the *Leonardo* to the *Erasmus* programme and to set up a single programme committee to oversee the whole programme should contribute positively to the overall coherence of the programmes and the harmonisation and simplification of the procedures.**

209. **We recommend, however, that the Commission should explain in greater detail how these changes are intended to work.**

210. **We also recommend that these changes should be subjected to a stringent mid-term review in which the views of all relevant stakeholders are consulted and full taken into account.**

CHAPTER 12: TRANSVERSAL PROGRAMME

211. This curiously-named innovation appears to be seen by the Commission as the key-stone to the architecture of their integrated approach. We understand that it is designed to link the sectoral programmes with cross-cutting elements, the need for which was identified during the Commission's interim evaluations of the *Socrates* and *Leonardo* programmes[21].

212. The Transversal programme is divided into four so-called Key Activities:

   • Key Activity 1 would support policy development through existing systems such as CEDEFOP[22] and EURYDICE[23];

   • Key Activity 2 is described as being designed to complement "mainstream" language development in the sectoral programmes through activities such as multilateral projects to develop and test language-learning methods and tools, networks of expertise and ICT resources and awareness-raising campaigns;

   • Key Activity 3 would focus on innovative approaches to teaching and learning through ICT; and,

   • Key Activity 4 would be mainly concerned with disseminating information and transferring good project results into educational and vocational training systems[24].

213. The operational objectives in *Article 37* of the proposed Decision adds the following specific requirements to these broad definitions:

   • "to ensure an adequate supply of comparable data, statistics and analyses to underpin lifelong learning policy development"; and to,

   • "monitor progress towards objectives and targets in lifelong learning, and to identify areas for particular attention"[25].

214. The Commission told us that, since much of the management of the new programme would be devolved to national agencies, the Transversal programme was intended to ensure that "people are not reinventing the wheel", and that key developments in language-learning and ICT were properly supported and coordinated (Q 43, Q 45, Q 53).

215. The Government saw the Transversal programme as a positive development. Activities covering several sectoral programmes should be properly promoted and coordinated without interfering with the national priorities of individual Member States (Q 19).

216. The British Council believed that bringing language-learning into the Transversal programme, where it would be allied to policy formation and

---

[21] 7210/04 COM (2004) 152 final and 7211/04 COM (2004) 153 final

[22] The European Centre for the development of Vocational Training based at Thessaloniki.

[23] Eurydice is a European information network for the exchange of educational information. It monitors processes and disseminates information on education systems and national policies through research units in participating countries (in the UK the National Foundation for Education Research –see written evidence at G43)

[24] 11587/04 COM 2004 474 final

[25] ibid

dissemination, should give it more prominence and potential impact (pp 11–16).

217. UUK welcomed the proposal, especially for stimulating curriculum development, university/enterprise links, and language and ICT development, so long as "these are more adequately funded than previous curriculum initiatives" and tailored to national circumstances (pp 60–64).

218. The Welsh Assembly Government hoped that the Transversal programme would allow projects to work across age ranges or help in bridging academic and vocational and formal and informal training. They commented "such an approach would be wholly consistent with the seamless, cradle-to-grave ethos of lifelong learning" and give ICT development more support than if it were subsumed within sectoral programmes (pp 295–299).

219. The EURYDICE Unit at the National Foundation for Education Research believed that the Transversal programme would consolidate and improve the network's central contribution towards the achievement of Lisbon goals (G43).

220. The Learning and Skills Council welcomed the focus on language-learning in the *Transversal* programme proposals which could make an important contribution to the National Languages Strategy (Q 446).

221. The following example, drawn from written evidence from CILT, the National Centre for Languages, (pp 225–228) illustrates projects currently funded through *Socrates* and *Leonardo* programmes involving ICT and language teaching and learning which might be covered by the proposed *Transversal* programme in the future.

BOX 10

Support for language teaching and learning

The National Centre for Languages has been funded through Socrates and Leonardo for a series of innovative projects:

Intercultural Competence Assessment: developed a framework for assessing intercultural competence for the engineering sector, with transferability to other sectors

Linguanet Europa: development of a multilingual resource centre for languages, currently accessed by 6000 users per month.

Language Research Centre project: working with European partners operating resource centres for languages and developing good practice in organisation and management.

ILIAD (International Languages Inservice at a Distance). A collaboration with the Open University created a multilingual, multimedia training resource for language teachers comparing approaches and practices across Europe.

222. Other evidence supported the proposal in principle, but indicated that the organisations concerned wanted to know more about how it would work in practice. (Q 196, pp 229–230, pp 267–269)

223. We were particularly struck by the evidence of the Open University (p 270) which advocated using properly-supported multi-media distance-learning systems to overcome constraints on mobility and enable programmes to reach out to wider and less-mobile potential participants at relatively low

cost. This is a field where the United Kingdom has a well-proven and highly successful track record on which we would hope that the Transversal programme could draw with advantage.

224. **We conclude that the *Transversal* programme is a potentially positive innovation, although many of the details of how it is intended to work in practice are as yet unclear. We support the Commission's stated aims of improving policy development, dissemination of good practice and enabling projects to bridge sectoral strands, and welcome the specific emphasis on improving standards of language and ICT training and development through cross-programme co-ordination.**

225. **We also conclude that if it is to work effectively the *Transversal* programme will need to be adequately funded and properly managed. On the other hand, we are concerned that it should not impose unnecessary bureaucracy or interfere with the proper responsibilities of participating countries.**

226. **Here again, therefore, we recommend that the Commission should provide a more detailed explanation than we have seen so far of how this programme is intended to work in practice which should be subjected to careful examination by the Member States in Council.**

227. **We further recommend that the Commission should study and make recommendations to Council on how the *Transversal* programme might incorporate and disseminate the experience gained by successful distance-learning providers, such as the Open University in the United Kingdom, in designing innovative learning packages that would help to make the benefits of the programme more widely available to those with limited or no mobility.**

228. **Here too, we also recommend and that the programme should be subjected to a stringent mid-term review in which the views of all relevant stakeholders are consulted and fully taken into account.**

CHAPTER 13: SIMPLIFICATION

229. The Commission acknowledged pressure from Member States, national agencies and public consultations, as well as within the Commission itself, for simpler and more flexible programmes. It stated that simplification required more than good intentions: the legislative environment had to be appropriate; where it was not the necessary legislative derogation should be introduced. The guiding principle should be proportionality: the administrative and accounting requirements should be proportional to the size of the grant. [26]

230. It proposed the following improvements:

- greater use of flat-rate grants and scales of unit costs;

- simpler application forms and contracts;

- extending co-financing through contributions in kind, and limiting the accounting obligations of beneficiaries in such cases; and,

- simplified documentation on the financial and operational capacity of beneficiaries.

231. Where necessary, it said appropriate derogations to the Financial Regulations would be presented.[27]

232. The Commission also proposed that more activities should be managed through national agencies because they understood the national context and priorities and had "the ability to create a more user-friendly environment".

233. The Commission's interim evaluations of the *Leonardo* and Socrates programmes[28] each reported that, despite simplification and greater decentralisation, users continued to complain about cumbersome and time-consuming bureaucracy.

234. These complaints were, to some extent, related to the introduction in 2003 of the new Financial Regulations. Complaints included far too much information being required for project applications and monitoring and procedural delays.

235. The Commission told us they hoped that integration of the programme would enable them to ease the financial and administrative regulations. They were well aware of the burden which these placed on participants, as well as on national agencies and the Commission themselves. But, for the moment, the Financial Regulations were "part of the legislation and until, therefore, the legislation is changed it is impossible for us to make major simplifications" (Q 43).

236. We were also told that, while it might not be possible under the present rules to achieve significant simplification for national agencies, the Commission hoped that it might be achieved for final beneficiaries such as schools and universities (Q 59).

---

[26] 11587/04 COM (2004) 474 final

[27] ibid

[28] 7210/04 COM (2004) 152 final and 7211/04 COM (2004) 153 final

237. The Government told us they welcomed the proposal for greater decentralisation. They were seeking clarification on how decentralisation would work in practice to ensure that it made running programmes more cost-effective while ensuring appropriate accountability (Q 145).

238. The British Council took the view that:

- "the aims will not be met, nor will the ambitious participation targets be achieved, if the new Financial Regulations and Implementing Rules are continued as they currently stand. The principle of proportionality must be applied to enable the small-scale, grass roots projects to flourish and to increase the impact of the programmes on the United Kingdom education constituencies" and that,

- "aspects of financial management… must be commensurate with a level of grant applied for and consistent with national statutory requirements for financial reporting" (pp 11–16).

239. They added that much less bureaucracy and much less onerous reporting regulations were essential if the programme were to become truly inclusive. The bureaucratic requirements for schools receiving a few thousand euros were not dissimilar for those imposed on institutions receiving a hundred times as much (Q 39).

240. As has already been noted in preceding chapters, we received numerous complaints in evidence about the bureaucratic burden caused by the present administrative procedures. These included:

- although the management arrangements for *Leonardo* had been simplified, the documentation was still lengthy and complex and the management element available under the grant was insufficient to cover universities' administrative costs. This was deterring some universities from applying. More flexible and less onerous rules were needed (QQ 119–121);

- a disproportionate amount of time was spent in accounting for minor expenses. The travel rules were too inflexible (QQ 164–167);

- the *Leonardo* application process was equally complex and long-winded and the frequent detailed audit reports were excessive and disproportionate to the sums involved. They imposed unfair burdens on smaller colleges and voluntary organisations, deterring some from taking part (QQ 199–200, Q 231, QQ 243–244, QQ 295–296);

- the inflexibility of the bidding timetable for applications also posed intolerable burdens for small organisations (Q 240, Q 243);

- the *Leonardo* and *Comenius* travel budgets were inadequate, especially for those travelling from remoter locations (Q 298, Q 388);

- the *Comenius* application process also involved considerable form filling. It might be simplified by allowing schools to submit a full application once in three years with a simpler annual re-application procedure in the intervening years (Q 367);

- lack of adequate revenue, compared with the income generated by international student recruitment had caused EU-funded work to remain at the margins at many universities (pp 262–264); and,

- the *Leonardo* and *Socrates* administrative processes were incompatible. *Leonardo* was seen as more administratively burdensome than *Socrates*. Simpler processes would improve participation and engender innovation (pp 270–271).

241. The United Kingdom Socrates-Erasmus Council agreed that universities found the management cost provision for mobility programmes to be insufficient. Although bureaucratic requirements had been reduced and national agencies did their best to help, the reporting burden was still quite considerable for hard-pressed institutions (Q 172).

242. The United Kingdom Socrates-Erasmus Council also feared that the introduction of the clumsily-named system of *Indirect Centralised Management* might reinforce the tendency for the Commission to micromanage. The procedure was "very detailed and highly prescriptive" and was likely to make a substantial difference to the way that national agencies operated. The Commission, Member States and national agencies were still trying to grapple with the implications.

243. The Council described the new Financial Regulation and implementing rules as "fairly impenetrable". The rules appeared to be designed for massive sums available under Structural Funds and were inappropriate for the relatively small sums of money involved in these programmes and the type of institutions that would have to deal with them (Q 174, pp 90–97).

244. Bureaucracy is obviously the Achilles heel of current programmes. We welcome the Commission's commitment to simplify procedures and decentralise more decision-making to national agencies. But it is evident that the new Financial Regulations introduced late in the current programme are acting as a disincentive to some potential participants and causing excessive and unfair burdens, especially on small and medium-sized organisations.

245. **We recommend that every effort should be made by the Commission to apply the principle of proportionality to all funding applications and other administrative and financial procedures under this programme, especially to enable small scale grass-roots projects to flourish and to encourage smaller organisations to believe that they have a realistic chance of taking part in these programmes.**

246. **We also recommend that more adequate funding should be earmarked to cover the staff costs for organising, managing and supporting mobility projects, and the additional travel costs of those in remoter areas. The Commission should also investigate other ways of making the funding rules more flexible and better-tailored to the circumstances of potential participants without eroding proper accountability.**

247. **We further recommend that the Commission, working with national agencies, should strive to ease the burden on smaller participating organisations by introducing more user-friendly software, help lines, training seminars and arrangements for sharing advice from experienced participants.**

CHAPTER 14: FUNDING

248. One of the most striking aspects of the new programme is the proposed budget. The total figure of €13.620 billion for the period 2007–2013 is more than three and a half times the total budget for the current programmes.

249. The cost justification in the Commission's Extended Impact Assessment (EIA) [29] includes the statement:

"the level of intervention could not be lowered without running the risk of reducing the programmes' impact to such a low level that the European added value would be entirely lost. The targeted ambitions are measured so as to make it possible to influence educational and training systems in a credible way and so as to meet the citizens' expectations."

250. The EIA goes on to say that past experience has shown that "retaining the rhetoric of education and training programmes" without providing adequate resources has proved to be a weakness and resulted in failure to achieve the desired impact. It claims that "the present proposal has carefully estimated the cost of reaching its objectives"[30].

251. It also lays stress on the importance of expanding mobility programmes, which are expensive to administer, and points to the limited potential for participating organisations to increase co-financing. But it claims that the average individual cost for each project is proportionately low in relation to the expected results. The Commission told us that the estimated costs amounted to "the minimum if we are to respond to the expectations put on the programme and put on education and training activities" by the Lisbon, Bologna and Copenhagen declarations (Q 42).

252. As already noted in Chapter 3, the Government's position is that any decision on the budget will have to wait until the negotiations on the new Financial Perspective have been agreed (Q21, pp 1–6). The Minister of State for Lifelong Learning, Further and Higher Education at the Department for Education and Skills, Dr Kim Howells, (the Minister) told us he thought it was very difficult to see how the budget could be increased by three and a half times without a very clear idea of how the money would be spent. The Government would be looking for evidence-based policies and value for money (Q 503).

253. In the time available we have not been able to attempt a detailed assessment of the validity of the estimates produced by the Commission. Nor have these been subjected to any detailed examination by our witnesses. We therefore find it difficult to judge whether these estimates are reasonable.

254. Given the Government's position on the Financial Perspective, we do not expect to be able to give more detailed consideration to the budget until the negotiations on the Financial Perspective have been concluded and the Government has reported back to us on the resultant negotiations with the Commission on the detailed budgetary aspects of these proposals.

255. **We conclude that, for the moment and for the purposes of this Report, we are unable to judge whether the estimated budget of €13.620 billion for the proposed programme is reasonable. We hope to**

---

[29] Commission Staff Working Paper: Extended Impact Assessment 11587/04 COM (2004) 474 final

[30] ibid

be able to consider this in more detail once the negotiations on the Financial Perspective have been concluded and the Government have reported back to us on the outcome.

256. At this stage, however, we would observe that an increase of more than 3.5 times the present budget will require searching investigation and convincing justification. We accept that a substantial increase in the volume and scope of the present programmes will be needed if the ambitious goals set by the Lisbon process are to be attained. We have also noted evidence that some of the existing grants, especially those related to the costs of administering the programmes and ensuring that the programmes are truly inclusive, are inadequate and will need to be remedied in the new programme.

257. Nevertheless, as we have already concluded, some of the targets proposed by the Commission are very ambitious and our evidence leads us to doubt whether all of them can realistically be achieved within the time set.

258. We recommend that these factors should be borne carefully in mind as the proposed budget comes to be examined and we fully support the Government's intention to probe these estimates for value for money.

259. We also recommend that the Commission should consider whether, in an understandable desire to increase participation, the proposed funds may be spread too thinly and fail to improve some of the funding deficiencies which have prevented the present programmes from being fully effective and reaching more disadvantaged people.

CHAPTER 15: ROLE OF THE BRITISH GOVERNMENT

United Kingdom Government Strategy

260. The preceding chapters have examined the lessons to be learned from present EU education and training programmes and the extent to which those lessons appear to have been taken into account in framing the new proposals. The recommendations we have made in those chapters are directed initially at the Commission. But they are also directed at the United Kingdom Government which has the responsibility for negotiating improvements and clarifications to the Proposal over the coming months, and especially during the forthcoming period of the United Kingdom Presidency.

261. **We recommend that the United Kingdom Government should consider carefully the preceding recommendations and urge the Commission in negotiations during the coming months to amend or clarify the existing Proposal to give effect to those recommendations.**

262. **We regard the United Kingdom Government as having a special responsibility to take the lead in supporting those recommendations and ensuring a satisfactory outcome during the forthcoming United Kingdom Presidency of the EU.**

263. At the same time, our evidence has indicated several areas where specific national action appears to be needed to remedy problems of a national nature identified by the evidence and to make sure that the United Kingdom makes the best possible use of the opportunities presented by the new programme.

264. At a policy level, witnesses from the higher education sector claimed that until relatively recently the Government had focused mainly on national education needs and had not paid enough attention to the European dimension. They pointed out that the Government's Higher Education White Paper in 2003 had not mentioned Europe at all. They contended that United Kingdom policy makers had not taken the links between United Kingdom higher education policy, the Bologna process and Erasmus programme   seriously   enough (Q 100, Q 128, Q 135, Q 179 and pp 77–80).

265. Witnesses from further education and adult education colleges complained about what they saw as a lack of overall coherent national strategy and inadequate connections between the delivery of the programmes by colleges, the national agency and policy makers in the Departments (QQ 191–192).One witness described the position as "there is no encouragement but there is also no discouragement; it is left to the individual colleges" (Q 224).

266. But witnesses acknowledged that Government attitudes appeared to have changed recently. The Government had been supportive of the setting up of a Europe Unit by the Higher Education sector (Q 100). Some witnesses welcomed the Department of Education new strategy document *"Putting the World into World Class Education"*[31] although it was felt that the policy statements in that document needed to be translated into a national action

---

[31] *"Putting the World into World Class Education"*, DfES Publication, ref. DfES/1077/2004

plan and that more recognition should be given to the work already being done by educational establishments (Q 195, pp 262–264).

267. Another witness suggested that the Foster Inquiry into further education should be encouraged to look closely at what needed to be done to make the national response to opportunities presented by the programme more effective (Q 195).

268. It was also suggested that the European dimension should be embedded in the national curriculum (Q 250). The Government should carry out a strategic planning exercise to consider the programme proposals and the resources made available (Q 137).

269. Witnesses dealing with the *Comenius* programme pointed out that although the new international strategy advocated that every school should have an international partnership and work towards the International School Award, it said nothing about how that should happen or about the capacity of LEAs to deliver the objective (Q 320, Q 361).

270. Although some LEAs have encouraged the development of international links, our evidence indicates that the picture is patchy at best (Q 320, Q 333) Witnesses suggested that this partly explained why the national average of schools taking part in *Comenius* projects is only about 1 in 25 (QQ 333–342).

271. Witnesses advocated that the Government should do more to give a lead to LEAs through the Standards Fund and the Ofsted inspection process to encourage more schools to take part in *Comenius* and that those schools and teachers which made the effort to do so should be given more recognition and support. (Q 286, Q 342, Q 365, QQ 393–396).

272. We asked witnesses whether the Learning and Skills Councils or Regional Development Agencies (RDAs) played any part in developing United Kingdom strategies for making the most of these programmes or helping those who were taking part in them. On the whole, apart from some assistance in Scotland from Local Enterprise Companies, witnesses thought they did not (Q 198, Q 232, QQ 251–254).

273. The Learning and Skills Council (LSC) told us that they were represented on the United Kingdom Leonardo Advisory Group, but were not otherwise directly involved with any of the programmes. They tended to concentrate on European Social Fund (ESF). Local learning and skills councils were sometimes involved in helping individual programmes (QQ 412–423). But the LSC had no dialogue with the DfES about new education and training programmes. They said they would welcome closer involvement and thought their experience with the ESF would be useful (Q 428).

274. According to the LSC, the RDAs worked very closely with them in developing the Skills Strategy and using Structural Funds. The LSC thought that as regional skills partnerships developed the RDAs could help to make employers aware of the opportunities presented by the *Leonardo* and *Grundtvig* programmes and might support them where projects were relevant to regional skills priorities (Q 432).

275. We asked the Minister about witnesses' perception of lack of a coherent United Kingdom strategy to guide and support the programmes and the variable support apparently available from Local Education Authorities. He told us that, on taking office, his Department had been obliged to give priority to domestic education problems, especially lack of literacy, numeracy

and other basic skills. He added "although I think we genuflected towards the altar of these great pan-European programmes, they were not really at the heart of the Government policies at that time. We recognised their importance and there were lots of people, especially at the universities and schools who were engaged in the exchange programmes. I think they seemed to us at the time to be taking care of themselves. It was ticking along nicely. We did not need really to get particularly involved in that" (Q 467).

276. But the Minister pointed out that in the past six months the Department had published a new international strategy. In the past, successive Governments had left it to individual schools and colleges to make the running. The Government now understood it was not possible to have a single educational policy that could exist separately from the European dimension. Even so, tough decisions had to be made. Far more European apprentices wanted to come to the United Kingdom than British apprentices wanted to go to Europe. Schools and universities were pursuing huge opportunities in the global education marketplace outside Europe, for example in China (QQ 467, 469).

277. We are grateful for the Minister's assurances, as far as they go, but we are still not clear how much priority the Government attaches to these programmes nor how the Government's new international strategy will be developed. We are concerned by the impressions so many of our witnesses have formed of past Government neglect and lack of strategy.

278. **We conclude that, while the encouragement given to participation in the EU education and training programmes in the Government's recent publication *Putting the World into World-Class Education* is welcome, it is regrettable that the Government does not appear to have paid much attention to the importance of these programmes, or given much support or encouragement to participants, in the past. We also regret that witnesses from across the spectrum of the education and training sectors are still unclear about the Government's strategy for these programmes and the degree of priority which the Government attaches to them.**

279. **We recommend that the Government should publish as soon as possible a clear statement of the priority which they attach to EU education and training programmes and outline in more detail their current thinking about the new programme.**

280. **We further recommend that the Government should then embark on an urgent consultation with representatives of all sectors of education in this country, as well as with Local Education Authorities, the Learning Skills Councils and the Regional Development Agencies and other interested bodies, with a view to drawing up a clear public strategy for maximising the opportunities presented by the new programme, eliminating unnecessary barriers and identifying how those consulted might best contribute to that strategy.**

CHAPTER 16: BARRIERS TC ___ DM INVOLVEMENT

281. We have drawn attention in pr... ...vidence we have been given about seeming inadequacies ... ...'s present arrangements for funding participation in these programmes. But it is apparent from our evidence that some of these shortcomings have been exacerbated by conditions peculiar to the United Kingdom.

282. In Chapter 6 we noted two potentially disturbing trends in the evidence supplied by the United Kingdom Socrates-Erasmus Council:

- United Kingdom participation in *Erasmus* student mobility has declined since the peak of 12,000 in 1994–1995. In 2003/2004 the United Kingdom total was 7,539 compared with rising totals from France (20981), Spain (20034), Germany (20688) and Italy (16383). Outward United Kingdom *Erasmus* mobility to the new partner countries, especially east and central Europe, was also particularly low (only 229 in 2002/2003) (pp 90–97); and,

- moreover, the United Kingdom is no longer the most popular destination for *Erasmus* students. In 2003-2004 16427 Erasmus students came to the United Kingdom making it the third most popular destination after Spain (21306) and France (18822) (pp 90–97).

283. This is further illustrated by the charts in Figures 3 and 4 showing the relative flows of Erasmus students from Germany, Spain, France and the United Kingdom in 2002–2003, compared with 1995–1996.

FIGURE 4

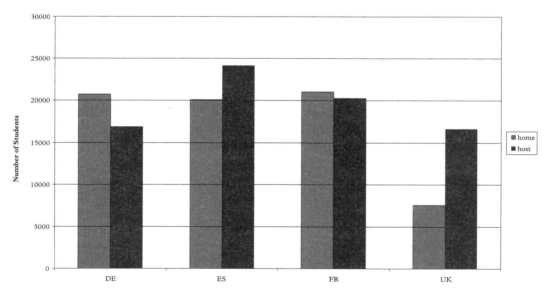

Flows of Erasmus Students 2003-2004

FIGURE 5

Flows of Erasmus Students 1995-96

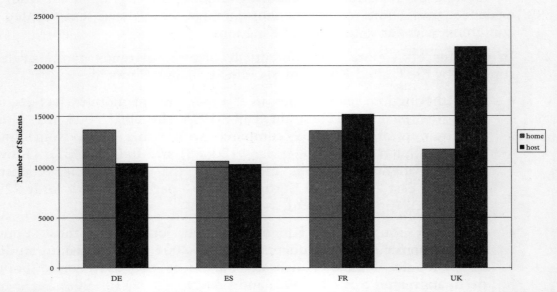

284. The United Kingdom Socrates-Erasmus Council told us that a recent HEFCE study had suggested that the main reasons for declining United Kingdom participation were declining language competence, financial problems and lack of motivation (Q 179, pp 90–97). The culture in other European countries embraced the objective of mobility to a greater extent than in the United Kingdom and *Erasmus* was much better promoted there. United Kingdom universities were keen on encouraging incoming students but it was "not on the agenda to promote outward mobility". Too much depended on individual enthusiasts (Q 179).

285. The Council argued that it was absolutely critical for the future of Britain to have a generation of young people imbued with multicultural ideas who were able to mix and network effectively with their peers in other European countries. United Kingdom participation in *Erasmus* had not kept pace with the growth of higher education (QQ 179–180). Much more public attention needed to be given to the opportunities through a properly-funded promotion campaign (Q 184).

286. We asked witnesses from the universities about this. UUK reiterated that financial support for students and institutions had been inadequate. The next generation of programmes must be better supported and the costs of administration fully recompensed. Universities had "no slack in the system" to subsidise these programmes. It was critically important that both the Commission and the Government should provide appropriate funding, as well as reducing administrative burdens (Q 65).

287. Moreover, UUK pointed out that students with sufficient language skills were in short supply. More also needed to be done to help students from poorer backgrounds with part-time work or family commitments to overcome practical constraints on participation (Q 65). The programmes' opportunities had been provided at an increasing cost in time, money and physical resources to United Kingdom institutions and their staff because of the inadequacies and complexities of funding. Moreover, the changing nature

of the United Kingdom student population meant that year-long mobility programmes were less attractive than in the past (QQ 70–74). The majority of United Kingdom students taking Erasmus placements were language students, whereas incoming Erasmus students were studying a much wider range of disciplines (Q 90).

288. UUK also noted an increasing trend for Continental European universities to run courses in English. It was part of the increasingly competitive global market for international students. This was attractive to British students who lacked the necessary competence in European languages. But it also meant that United Kingdom no longer had a competitive edge in attracting foreign students (QQ 92-94). At the same time, British universities were having to restrict the numbers of foreign students coming to the United Kingdom under *Erasmus* programmes because they incurred an extra cost for which no funding was provided by the programme (Q 102).

289. UACES agreed that because universities were highly dependant on fee income they had little incentive to take part in cooperative European activities like *Erasmus*. They claimed this was partly because the Government viewed higher education as a service or trade (QQ 135–136). Reduced United Kingdom participation in *Erasmus* was directly related to the funding structure of universities (QQ 138 – 141). Competition from Continental European universities offering courses in high-quality English was growing. Some of them were very close to United Kingdom standards of quality, but their fees tended to be much lower (Q 141).

290. UACES reiterated that a major reason for the United Kingdom falling to third place as a destination of choice for foreign *Erasmus* students was because, under present funding arrangements, many British universities could not afford to take any more (Q 146). Changing Continental attitudes towards the learning of English also meant that Continental European academics and students were better prepared to take advantage of British further education. They realised that English was no longer a language but more of a tool like using a computer or driving a car (Q 149).

291. We asked the Minister about these trends. He pointed out that more British students were studying abroad than ever. But more were tending to go to the USA and Australia, which had a more glamorous and dynamic image as well as some very good universities. United Kingdom language capability was a real problem. If the decline in the British language teaching was not arrested, the decline in participation in programmes like *Erasmus* was likely to grow (Q 480).

292. The Minister considered that the growth in the popularity of learning English internationally was only one factor. Worries about student loans might be deterring some British students from applying for *Erasmus* placements. The strong pound also tended to deter foreign students from coming to this country to study (QQ 482–485).

293. But the Minister assured us that he was keen to reverse the trend towards declining United Kingdom participation (Q 483). British universities and students needed more access to the important work being done by Continental academics and to overcome complacency about the quality of university provision in the United Kingdom (Q 483).

294. We asked the Minister about the claims that the funding allocation did not cover the cost of administering programmes adequately. He replied that an

administration grant was paid to higher education institutions and colleges to help them cover the costs of organising mobility. These institutions were autonomous bodies and could choose to use that money as they saw fit, as well using money from other sources. The Government was prevented by law from telling HEFCE and universities how they should spend their money. But he admitted that the Government "could probably have a much more vigorous discussion than we have had with higher education institutions about the benefits of taking part in these courses". Departmental officials were discussing the problem of administration cost provision with HEFCE and universities (Q 489).

295. UUK have since challenged the Minister's statement. They point out that institutions must account very rigorously for the small grants they receive for the organisation of mobility. They claimed that all universities taking part in the programmes would be supporting mobility programmes by cross-subsidising from other sources, especially the unfunded participation of incoming students whose numbers currently exceeded the number of outgoing EU-supported students. They argued that it was wrong to suggest that universities might be choosing to spend EU resources on other activities. They gave us further examples of what they saw as the inadequate funding of grants for organising mobility grants and of the bureaucratic difficulties involved in running these programmes (pp 215–217).

296. We also asked the Minister about the lack of supply cover for teachers taking part in Comenius programmes, which had been raised with us by several witnesses. The Minister confirmed that the cost of paying for a supply teacher was not recoverable under EU funding rules. But he said that the British Council had increased the subsistence allowance in the 2004 contract to encourage schools to support teacher mobility (Q 489).

297. We also asked the Minister to comment on the Commission's statement that United Kingdom under-spends on EU education and training programmes were higher than the EU average (Q 51). The Minister confirmed that the United Kingdom under-spend on *Comenius* and *Leonardo* programmes was currently above the European average. He hoped that the additional subsistence advance to schools would help (Q 489).

298. The Minister pointed out that the decline in the number of United Kingdom *Erasmus* students was not a proper reflection of the total number of British students studying in Europe. Over 4000 British students were studying independently in EU countries (Q 490). He admitted that the proportion of schools taking part in *Comenius* was small and added "I cannot decide in my own mind how serious it is". But the contribution which the programme made to learning of languages was undoubtedly an important factor for that reason alone he would like to see greater participation (Q 494).

299. The Minister also referred to the deadweight of bureaucracy as a significant deterrent to participation which the Government was determined to try to overcome (Q 499).

300. Although the Commission, the Government and the British Council all assured us that wider social inclusion and the needs of the disadvantaged were a high priority in these programmes, the evidence we have seen as indicated in earlier chapters shows that in the United Kingdom too much is left to individual initiative and determination in overcoming obstacles. It is also clear from the evidence, as noted in earlier chapters, that too much is left

to the same dedicated individuals to promote programmes and tackle bureaucratic problems.

301. **We recommend that the Government should carry out a systematic investigation, in consultation with educational institutions and other relevant bodies, into the reasons why United Kingdom participation in some of the present programmes, notably *Erasmus*, is decreasing and why the United Kingdom is no longer the first choice of destination for incoming *Erasmus* students from other participating countries.**

302. **We also recommend that the Government should investigate, in consultation with educational institutions and other relevant bodies, why United Kingdom under-spends on some of the current EU education and training programmes are more than those of other participating countries.**

303. **We further recommend that this investigation should pay particular attention to claims we have had in evidence that the current funding provision by the Commission is inadequate. The Government should establish to what extent that it due to institutional factors in the United Kingdom education system, as distinct from the rules and levels of funding set by the Commission.**

304. **The Government should also pay particular attention to the lack of supply cover for British teachers wishing to take part in *Comenius* programmes and any other factors peculiar to the United Kingdom which tend to discourage overall participation or exclude certain groups of potential beneficiaries.**

305. **We welcome the Government's assurances that they are committed to overcome the dead-weight of bureaucracy as a significant deterrent to participation in these programmes and to ensure that the programmes are genuinely inclusive. But it is clear to us from the evidence that the success of these programmes in the United Kingdom depends far too much on the dedication, hard work and resourcefulness of beleaguered individual enthusiasts. We recommend that the Government should ensure that they are given much more encouragement and support and demonstrate how they intend to do so.**

CHAPTER 17: LANGUAGES

306. The previous chapter has already noted that the decline in language competence was one of the main reasons for the fall in United Kingdom participation in the Erasmus programme. We wanted to know more about the underlying reasons for this decline.

307. The Government told us that the aim of the new DfES International Strategy was to transform national capability to learn and speak other languages. The National Languages Strategy for England highlighted the importance of languages to the cultural and linguistic richness of society, as well as to international trade and global citizenship. The Government therefore planned to offer language-learning from the age of seven, backed by high-quality teaching and learning opportunities. Although it would no longer be compulsory for students to study languages beyond age 14 (Key Stage 4), schools would still be required to offer language learning programmes to pupils who wanted to study a modern foreign language.

308. We were told that by the end of the decade every child would have had the opportunity to study a foreign language and develop an interest throughout Key Stage 2. The Government hoped that this would engender more enthusiasm for continuing with language learning. The Languages Strategy therefore depended on giving an earlier start to language learning, combined with a choice at later stages of school education. The Government did not see this as being inconsistent with the Barcelona objective that all school children should learn at least two foreign languages and pointed out that the United Kingdom was "not alone in having quite a long way to go towards achieving" that objective (QQ 25–26).

309. The Government also pointed to the large number of British *Erasmus* students who were working on modern language programmes as part of their courses abroad. But they added that surveys showed that many British students were worried that if they went abroad they would not necessarily benefit because they did not speak the relevant language. Students needed to be persuaded that they could benefit from *Erasmus* placements, even though they did not speak the language fluently at the start of their assignments. The Government believed that students would benefit from being exposed to another culture, regardless of their ability to speak the language. Nor did it necessarily follow that the increasing numbers of British students who chose to study in the USA or Australia did so because of lack of ability to speak foreign languages (QQ 28–29) The British Council told us that recognition of the importance of learning languages was growing, especially at primary school and colleges of further education, which should contribute to the Government's language strategy (Q 17).

310. The Commission endorsed the importance of delivering language-learning efficiently at primary school level in the hope of developing a sustained interest in languages at later stages in education. But this required well-trained teachers, specialising in teaching languages to very young children. It also required sufficient time in the curriculum, the appropriate materials and adequate support from parents as well as schools. An effective transition from primary to secondary language education was also essential (Q 51).

311. On the basis of current trends, UUK foresaw that British students would be less able to participate in programmes like *Erasmus*, as well as being less able

to secure employment abroad or with global companies, for some time to come. Recent studies showed that fewer than one third of state schools now required students to learn a language to the age of 16 and an increasing number of school pupils were dropping languages, especially in less advantaged areas and those schools with lower-than-average overall performance. This trend was also greater in the North than in the South. But universities were doing what they could, through their outreach to schools, to encourage language learning (Q 90).

312. UACES also welcomed the Government's plans to start more language-learning in primary schools but stressed how long it would take for that initiative to filter through to students. By the time the Commission's new programme was due to finish in 2013, the first of the British primary school children to benefit from the Government's initiative would still not have reached university level and the decline in school language learning would be reducing the potential pool of language teachers (Q 147).

313. Both UACES and the United Kingdom Socrates-Erasmus Council claimed that children from more privileged backgrounds tended to have better language training. This was reflected, to some extent, in the social mix of *Erasmus* students noted in the preceding chapter. UACES commented that without additional incentives, such as short "taster courses" to give potential students early intensive in-country language immersion "only the rich kids are going to do it" (Q 147 and Q 188).Without better preparation in languages, UACES agreed that young British people would be disadvantaged in the job market (Q 147).One college witness argued that every vocational course should have a language component (Q 250).

314. At school level, one of the advisers dealing with *Comenius* programmes told us that IT had been helpful in improving children's motivation to learn languages or think about the importance of language-learning, even though much of the communication with foreign schools was carried out in English (QQ 355–357). As noted in chapter 9, the teachers involved in *Comenius* projects who gave us evidence found that the interchange enhanced language-awareness and emphasised to pupils the importance of learning languages (Q 354, QQ 400–401).

315. The University Council of Modern Languages commented that "any ambition to widen *Socrates* participation beyond languages students is not likely to be achieved in the United Kingdom unless the Government is able to address the decline in languages take-up at secondary school level". This tended to hamper the extension of EU education and training programmes across social classes (pp 290–292).

316. The Head of the European Office at the University of Bristol also regretted the reduction in the requirement for language-teaching in secondary schools and considered that it was bound to affect participation in EU mobility programmes adversely, as well as having wider repercussions for the United Kingdom (G44).The national centre for languages CILT also called for more recognition that the United Kingdom needed to be better-equipped in the language competence in order to make full use of the funding available, especially under the *Erasmus* programme (pp 225–228). This was also emphasised by the United Kingdom Erasmus Student Committee (pp 90-97) and HEURO (pp 243– 256).

317. The Minister agreed with us that the decline in language teaching and learning in Britain was "a real problem" and that if it was not arrested it would be bound to affect United Kingdom participation in EU education and training programmes. But he cautioned against jumping to conclusions about recent Government decisions on language-teaching because all too often children who had been forced to learn languages had been discouraged from continuing with language studies. From the limited money available, the Government had decided to concentrate on the early years in the hope that the investment made would work through to an increase in demand for advanced language courses later on. He described this as "a statement of faith" (Q 480).

318. We are deeply disturbed by the evidence we have been given about the declining capacity for language-learning in this country. The consequences go well beyond the scope of this Inquiry and the programmes we are considering cannot do much to help redress the balance unless urgent and effective action is taken nationally to invest more in language-learning at all levels. It is to our national advantage that English is the generally-accepted international medium for communication. But that must not be seen as a substitute for the ability to communicate effectively in one or more other mainstream European languages which is essential if this country is to do business successfully in the widest sense with our European neighbours and with other countries where those languages are spoken.

319. **We conclude that the United Kingdom is already falling badly behind in language-learning capability. This will seriously limit British ability to take part fully in and benefit from the new EU programmes, especially *Erasmus*. But it has far wider implications for the employability and cultural awareness of the coming generation and will severely hamper the country's ability to protect and promote our interests abroad and to compete successfully in the Single Market and elsewhere.**

320. **We believe the problem will worsen as the new programme targets increasing proportions of the younger population. The United Kingdom will not be able to get anything like full value from the expanded EU programme proposed. While more funding for preparatory language training is a possible short-term solution, it will not address the more strategic deep-seated British linguistic deficiency which requires long-term commitment and investment to sustain improvement.**

321. **While we welcome the Government's intention to give more emphasis to early language-training in schools it will clearly be many years, stretching beyond the termination of the proposed new EU programme, before that has any effect on the capacity of young British adults to take advantage of EU-funded education and training schemes. It is also likely to lead to a short-fall in the number of language teachers needed to provide early language-teaching in schools and, in our view, the reduction in compulsory language learning at secondary level will only make matters worse.**

322. **We therefore recommend that the Government should carry out an urgent reappraisal of language teaching policy, not only for the implications it will have for United Kingdom participation in the new EU programme but much more widely.**

CHAPTER 18: UNITED KINGDOM BUSINESS ENGAGEMENT

323. From the outset we were anxious to have the views of the British business community on the relevance and quality of the existing EU education and training programmes and the extent to which the new programme proposals might offer business opportunities, contribute to the Lisbon competitiveness goals and meet the recruitment and training needs of British business. We therefore sent Calls for Evidence to a wide range of United Kingdom employer organisations, as well as to learning and skills councils, trades unions and every RDA.

324. While we were waiting for responses, the British Council told us that the business community was involved in the *Leonardo* programme. As the responsible national agency, the Council said they worked very closely with RDAs and sector skills councils to ensure that "business is as knitted into the programmes as is possible". Business was engaged in about 20 per cent of successful *Leonardo* projects and the CBI was represented on both the United Kingdom Leonardo and the Erasmus Councils and the Leonardo Advisory Group (Q35).

325. Nevertheless, the Council admitted that neither management nor trades unions had engaged with the programmes, or taken up the opportunities presented, as the Council would wish. Neither group had really addressed the issues of work-place learning in relation to the programmes. They thought this was probably partly because of the bureaucratic complexity of involvement in EU programmes. Until that was reduced it was doubtful whether British business would become more engaged (Q 33).

326. We have already noted in Chapter 7 the difficulties reported by colleges in attracting support from the business sector for *Leonardo* programmes (Q 235). But some witnesses had demonstrated that commercial support could be secured through good local contacts and effective personal promotion (QQ 236–237, Q 292, QQ 294–295).

327. We had written evidence from UNICE, the European Industrial and Employers Federation at an early stage. (pp 282–289) We have quoted from this evidence in preceding chapters. It broadly welcomes the contribution which the new programme can make to the Lisbon strategy and especially the aim to create a single, simple and more flexible life-long learning programme bringing education and training programmes together. But UNICE believed that simplifying and rationalising was not enough and called for a more outcome-focused approach to ensure that education and training policies would play their part in creating a competitive and dynamic knowledge-based society.

328. UNICE quotes from position paper published in February 2003 which called for the Commission to:

- tailor EU programme annual priorities and funding opportunities to real learning needs identified by companies and other social partners;

- focus EU programmes on supporting innovation and best practice;

- better identify and valorise (sic) good practice and disseminate project results; and

- simplify the procedures and reform the resources available.

329. It also called for closer consultation by the Commission with employer representatives at national and European level, including the Programme Management Committee (pp 282–289).

330. We have also noted in Chapter 7 the evidence from the Institution of Electrical Engineers which also called for more outcome-focused evaluation of *Leonardo* programmes, closer linkage with higher education and professional qualifications, and improved administrative arrangements to lessen the burden on smaller organisations and encourage them to participate more (pp 256–258). As noted in Chapter 15, the Learning and Skills Council gave us evidence which mainly concerned their extensive involvement with the ESF projects (QQ 411–463, pp 178–180).

331. In an attempt to secure a more comprehensive nationwide picture of employer's views, we reminded the CBI, the Institute of Directors, British Chambers of Commerce and the Federation of Small Businesses in January about our original Call for Evidence and invited them to consider giving oral evidence to the Inquiry, possibly in a collective session. They all declined, saying that they did not have enough direct experience of the programmes to offer useful evidence.

332. We were particularly surprised and disappointed at this reaction from the CBI, especially as we had been told that they represented British business interests on the United Kingdom Socrates-Erasmus Council and the United Kingdom Leonardo Advisory Group. Moreover, the CBI has often given valuable assistance to other Inquiries by this and other House of Lords Committees. The Chairman wrote accordingly to the Director-General of the CBI.

333. Sir Digby Jones replied that the CBI was committed to life-long learning and had worked at EU level in drawing up reports on the life-long development of competences and qualifications. But, although the CBI supported the ideals of programmes such as Erasmus and Leonardo, they were unable to offer any evidence on how those programmes had worked in practice, whether they offered good value for money, what lessons might be learned from them or what use the United Kingdom had made of them. He also stated that the CBI were no longer active on the United Kingdom Socrates-Erasmus Council, although they had helped to judge the Erasmus Student of the Year. This exchange of letters is printed in the Annex to the Report (pp 219–222).

334. **We recommend that the Government should encourage the United Kingdom business sector to pay more attention to the new Programme and the opportunities it may offer for British business and to become more actively engaged in helping the Government to develop their strategy towards the Programme, especially for the *Leonardo* and *Grundtvig* programmes.**

335. **At local level, we recommend that the Government should encourage businesses to liaise with the Regional Development Agencies and sector skills councils, as well as with individual local education institutions, in developing projects under this programme that are relevant to British business needs and will be of benefit to individual businesses and their employees.**

336. **We also recommend that the Government take more active steps to promote the potential benefits of the programme, and especially the**

new *Leonardo* and *Grundtvig* programmes to British business, not only for the training and motivation of individual employees, but also more widely through the corporate relationships and improved understanding of European processes and market opportunities which active involvement in these programmes should bring.

CHAPTER 19: UNITED KINGDOM NATIONAL AGENCY ARRANGEMENTS

337. As noted in Chapter 2, in the United Kingdom the British Council coordinates all aspects of the *Socrates* programme except for *Erasmus*, which is administered by the United Kingdom Socrates-Erasmus Council, and pilot schemes which are run by a commercial agency called ECOTEC.

338. Under the proposed new programme more responsibility will be devolved to national agencies. The Commission told us that, although the draft programme invited Member States to nominate one agency, several of the larger Member States felt that more than one agency was necessary (Q 45).

339. The evidence we have been given amply demonstrates a high level of confidence in, and satisfaction with, the present national agency arrangements in the United Kingdom. We respect those views and see no need to recommend changes, even though it is hard to see why a separate agency arrangement is necessary for running pilot projects.

340. On the other hand, the integrated aims of the new programme suggest that a more comprehensive approach may be necessary, with more active consultation by Government and the agencies of interested bodies such as education institutions, training organisations, employers, sector skills organisations, regional development agencies and trades unions.

341. To some extent that is already provided separately for the *Socrates* and *Leonardo* programmes by the relevant Advisory Councils. But we consider that those bodies should be unified to enable them to take a broad programme-wide view in advising Government on developing strategy and assessing performance. The day-to-day running of the individual programmes should be left to the agencies who seem to be doing it well.

342. **We recommend that the present agency arrangements for administering the programmes in the United Kingdom should be retained, but that consideration should be given to forming a single over-arching advisory council, on the lines of the present separate United Kingdom Socrates-Erasmus and Leonardo Advisory Councils, designed so that interested bodies can contribute effectively to the formation of a comprehensive national strategy and review progress while leaving programme administration in the hands of the relevant agencies.**

CHAPTER 20: FINAL RECOMMENDATION

343. **We commend this Report to the House and recommend that it should be debated by the House as soon as possible in the hope of drawing wider attention to the issues discussed in the Report and of influencing the European Commission and the Government in determining the final shape and details of the proposed programme.**

CHAPTER 21: CONCLUSIONS AND RECOMMENDATIONS

Competence and Subsidiarity

344. We conclude that the Commission's role in relation to these programmes is an appropriate one, and carried out with due respect for national competence.

345. Nevertheless, we recommend that the Member States in Council should continue to ensure that the Commission's plans and actions in developing this Proposal are appropriate, proportionate and fully consistent with the principle of subsidiarity.

Lisbon

346. We conclude that the proposed new Programme is broadly consistent with the Lisbon objective of making the EU a more competitive knowledge-based economy. It should make a positive contribution to that goal in the longer term. But, since the programme is not due to start until 2007, it cannot be expected to make much impact by 2010.

347. We recommend that the Programme should be seen as a long-term investment in building European capacity to prepare future generations for the challenges of globalisation and to enable the present working generation to improve and extend their skills.

Bologna

348. We conclude that, especially because of the emphasis on mobility, the proposed programme is broadly consistent with and should help to further the Bologna objectives. But it must be seen as a broad-based, long-term investment in life-long learning with a much wider range than higher education with which Bologna is concerned.

349. Nevertheless, between them the Lisbon and Bologna commitments do seem to us to represent a coherent and complementary policy framework for the proposed new programme.

Erasmus

350. We conclude that the priority given in the Proposal to the *Erasmus* programme is understandable and valid in principle. But we share the doubts expressed in evidence that the target to increase *Erasmus* student mobility to 3 million by 2011 is attainable.

351. We therefore recommend that the Commission should reassess that target and give serious consideration not only to the effect that the concentration on *Erasmus* may have on other programmes, but also on the need to ensure that students and institutions taking part in *Erasmus* are adequately funded and supported.

352. In doing so, we also recommend that the Commission should pay particular attention to the adequacy of the provision for the costs borne by institutions in organising *Erasmus* mobility.

353. We further recommend that the Commission should examine whether the present *Erasmus* programme is sufficiently inclusive and whether more ought

to be done through extra funding or more flexible rules to provide for more short-term mobility and to tailor programmes in other ways more closely to the reasonable needs of older and part-time students and those with work or family responsibilities.

354. We note that the present funding arrangements for *Erasmus* are based on an apparent assumption that roughly equivalent numbers of students would be exchanged between participating countries, which is clearly disadvantageous to the United Kingdom and some other participating countries. We recommend that the Commission should reconsider the theoretical assumptions which have led to this practice and bring forward proposals for a more equitable basis for funding.

355. We also recommend that the Commission should consider making the rules more flexible to allow for more post-graduate *Erasmus* placements and links with EU-funded research programmes.

356. We note the concern that has been raised with us that inconsistencies in the present European Credit Transfer System (ECTS) tend to put students at a disadvantage when carrying out *Erasmus*-funded study periods in other participating countries and to deter students from taking part in *Erasmus*. We recommend that the Commission should investigate these claims and report to Council on whether they are well-founded and, if so, what should be done about it.

Leonardo da Vinci

357. We conclude that the *Leonardo* programme is of considerable potential significance for the Lisbon agenda and appears, from the evidence we have been given, to have achieved a great deal in some cases. But much seems to depend on the admirable commitment and ingenuity of dedicated individuals in small organisations who lack adequate support.

358. We recommend that the Commission should examine the rules for the *Leonardo* programme to ensure that they are sufficiently flexible to meet the needs of part-time and older students and those with family responsibilities, as well as disadvantaged groups and those living in remoter areas.

359. The Commission should also examine whether the funding levels for the administration of *Leonardo* projects are adequate, especially for smaller colleges and non-profit organisations, and consider what else might be done to support such organisations and make their task easier.

360. We also recommend that more consideration should be given by the Commission to improving ways of disseminating good practice and spreading awareness of the positive benefits, especially for employers, of taking part in the *Leonardo* programme.

361. We further recommend that the Commission should examine the suggestion made to us that the match-funding requirements of this programme place an unfair burden on smaller tightly-funded organisations, and especially voluntary bodies, and that they ought to be changed.

Grundtvig

362. We conclude that the *Grundtvig* programme, like *Leonardo*, can make a significant contribution to the achievement of the Lisbon goals. *Grundtvig* is also an acid test of the Commission's commitment to genuine life-long

learning and, from the evidence we have been given, we are not convinced that the new *Grundtvig* programme is sufficiently well-tailored to the needs of older learners and the additional support they are likely to require.

363. We recommend that the Commission should give more consideration to demographic trends in Europe, as well as the inclusiveness and life-long learning aims of the overall programme. These factors suggest to us that more than the proposed 3% of the programme budget should be allocated to *Grundtvig* and we recommend that the Commission should re-examine the rationale for that allocation.

364. In framing the new packages for both *Leonardo* and *Grundtvig* we also recommend that the Commission should consider whether more innovative use of ICT and suitable distance-learning packages might help to overcome obstacles to participation, as well as encouraging improved computer capability for older participants.

Comenius

365. We conclude that *Comenius* is an important and imaginative programme with considerable potential which deserves more recognition and support.

366. We recommend that the Commission should look more closely at what needs to be done to encourage greater awareness and participation in *Comenius* and to remove unnecessary bureaucratic obstacles which impede effective participation and place unfair burdens on the dedicated organisers of these programmes, especially in smaller schools.

Value of the present Programmes

367. We conclude that the evidence we have been given, while anecdotal, amounts when taken together to a consistent, comprehensive and impressive picture of the value of these programmes. Despite some obvious shortcomings, the weight of evidence demonstrated to us significant improvement of individual skills, as well as character development, confidence-building and cultural awareness of those taking part. This should enhance the employability of individuals and contribute significantly to the overall European knowledge base, in-line with the Lisbon objectives.

368. We also conclude that participation in these programmes has enriched the lives of participants and contributed to the development of networks of useful cooperation between individuals and institutions in participating countries. Educational institutions in those countries have undoubtedly been strengthened, in-line with the Barcelona objectives.

369. We further conclude that the better understanding of the political, economic, commercial, historic and cultural significance of participating countries and European institutions which these programmes offer to those who take part in them, and the personal and institutional links that can be developed from them, should be of lasting value.

370. Nevertheless, we recommend that the Commission should consult with Member States and interested parties about the best way of devising a more systematic qualitative as well as quantitative analysis of the benefits and shortcomings of all the programmes for both the individuals and the institutions taking part, as well as for the wider benefits for the EU and other participating countries.

371. We further recommend that this analysis should be designed to inform future national strategies, as well as contributing to more effective dialogue between the Commission and participating countries about possible improvements whenever the programme is reviewed. But we believe it is essential that it should not add unduly to the bureaucratic burden on participants, especially from small organisations.

372. We also recommend that, having devised this system, the Commission should make sure that the results are widely disseminated in an easily-understandable format to Member State Governments, national agencies and both actual and potential participants in the programmes.

Integration

373. We conclude that the proposals to transfer vocational training at the higher education level from the *Leonardo* to the *Erasmus* programme and to set up a single programme committee to oversee the whole programme should contribute positively to the overall coherence of the programmes and the harmonisation and simplification of the procedures.

374. We recommend, however, that the Commission should explain in greater detail how these changes are intended to work.

375. We also recommend that these changes should be subjected to a stringent mid-term review in which the views of all relevant stakeholders are consulted and full taken into account.

Transversal Programme

376. We conclude that the *Transversal* programme is a potentially positive innovation, although many of the details of how it is intended to work in practice are as yet unclear. We support the Commission's stated aims of improving policy development, dissemination of good practice and enabling projects to bridge sectoral strands, and welcome the specific emphasis on improving standards of language and ICT training and development through cross-programme co-ordination.

377. We also conclude that if it is to work effectively the *Transversal* programme will need to be adequately funded and properly managed. On the other hand, we are concerned that it should not impose unnecessary bureaucracy or interfere with the proper responsibilities of participating countries.

378. Here again, therefore, we recommend that the Commission should provide a more detailed explanation than we have seen so far of how this programme is intended to work in practice which should be subjected to careful examination by the Member States in Council.

379. We further recommend that the Commission should study and make recommendations to Council on how the *Transversal* programme might incorporate and disseminate the experience gained by successful distance-learning providers, such as the Open University in the United Kingdom, in designing innovative learning packages that would help to make the benefits of the programme more widely available to those with limited or no mobility.

380. Here too, we also recommend and that the programme should be subjected to a stringent mid-term review in which the views of all relevant stakeholders are consulted and fully taken into account.

Simplification

381. We recommend that every effort should be made by the Commission to apply the principle of proportionality to all funding applications and other administrative and financial procedures under this programme, especially to enable small scale grass-roots projects to flourish and to encourage smaller organisations to believe that they have a realistic chance of taking part in these programmes.

382. We also recommend that more adequate funding should be earmarked to cover the staff costs for organising, managing and supporting mobility projects, and the additional travel costs of those in remoter areas. The Commission should also investigate other ways of making the funding rules more flexible and better-tailored to the circumstances of potential participants without eroding proper accountability.

383. We further recommend that the Commission, working with national agencies, should strive to ease the burden on smaller participating organisations by introducing more user-friendly software, help lines, training seminars and arrangements for sharing advice from experienced participants.

Funding

384. We conclude that, for the moment and for the purposes of this Report, we are unable to judge whether the estimated budget of euro 13.620 billion for the proposed programme is reasonable. We hope to be able to consider this in more detail once the negotiations on the Financial Perspective have been concluded and the Government have reported back to us on the outcome.

385. At this stage, however, we would observe that an increase of more than 3.5 times the present budget will require searching investigation and convincing justification. We accept that a substantial increase in the volume and scope of the present programmes will be needed if the ambitious goals set by the Lisbon process are to be attained. We have also noted evidence that some of the existing grants, especially those related to the costs of administering the programmes and ensuring that the programmes are truly inclusive, are inadequate and will need to be remedied in the new programme.

386. Nevertheless, as we have already concluded, some of the targets proposed by the Commission are very ambitious and our evidence leads us to doubt whether all of them can realistically be achieved within the time set.

387. We recommend that these factors should be borne carefully in mind as the proposed budget comes to be examined and we fully support the Government's intention to probe these estimates for value for money.

388. We also recommend that the Commission should consider whether, in an understandable desire to increase participation, the proposed funds may be spread too thinly and fail to improve some of the funding deficiencies which have prevented the present programmes from being fully effective and reaching more disadvantaged people.

Role of the British Government

389. We recommend that the United Kingdom Government should consider carefully the preceding recommendations and urge the Commission in negotiations during the coming months to amend or clarify the existing Proposal to give effect to those recommendations.

390. We regard the United Kingdom Government as having a special responsibility to take the lead in supporting those recommendations and ensuring a satisfactory outcome during the forthcoming United Kingdom Presidency of the EU.

391. We conclude that, while the encouragement given to participation in the EU education and training programmes in the Government's recent publication *Putting the World into World-Class Education* is welcome, it is regrettable that the Government does not appear to have paid much attention to the importance of these programmes, or given much support or encouragement to participants, in the past. We also regret that witnesses from across the spectrum of the education and training sectors are still unclear about the Government's strategy for these programmes and the degree of priority which the Government attaches to them.

392. We recommend that the Government should publish as soon as possible a clear statement of the priority which they attach to EU education and training programmes and outline in more detail their current thinking about the new programme.

393. We further recommend that the Government should then embark on an urgent consultation with representatives of all sectors of education in this country, as well as with Local Education Authorities, the Learning Skills Councils and the Regional Development Agencies and other interested bodies, with a view to drawing up a clear public strategy for maximising the opportunities presented by the new programme, eliminating unnecessary barriers and identifying how those consulted might best contribute to that strategy.

Barriers to United Kingdom involvement

394. We recommend that the Government should carry out a systematic investigation, in consultation with educational institutions and other relevant bodies, into the reasons why United Kingdom participation in some of the present programmes, notably *Erasmus*, is decreasing and why the United Kingdom is no longer the first choice of destination for incoming *Erasmus* students from other participating countries.

395. We also recommend that the Government should investigate, in consultation with educational institutions and other relevant bodies, why United Kingdom under-spends on some of the current EU education and training programmes are more than those of other participating countries.

396. We further recommend that this investigation should pay particular attention to claims we have had in evidence that the current funding provision by the Commission is inadequate. The Government should establish to what extent that it due to institutional factors in the United Kingdom education system, as distinct from the rules and levels of funding set by the Commission.

397. The Government should also pay particular attention to the lack of supply cover for British teachers wishing to take part in *Comenius* programmes and any other factors peculiar to the United Kingdom which tend to discourage overall participation or exclude certain groups of potential beneficiaries.

398. We welcome the Government's assurances that they are committed to overcome the dead-weight of bureaucracy as a significant deterrent to participation in these programmes and to ensure that the programmes are

genuinely inclusive. But it is clear to us from the evidence that the success of these programmes in the United Kingdom depends far too much on the dedication, hard work and resourcefulness of beleaguered individual enthusiasts. We recommend that the Government should ensure that they are given much more encouragement and support and demonstrate how they intend to do so.

Languages

399. We conclude that the United Kingdom is already falling badly behind in language-learning capability. This will seriously limit British ability to take part fully in and benefit from the new EU programmes, especially *Erasmus*. But it has far wider implications for the employability and cultural awareness of the coming generation and will severely hamper the country's ability to protect and promote our interests abroad and to compete successfully in the Single Market and elsewhere.

400. We believe the problem will worsen as the new programme targets increasing proportions of the younger population. The United Kingdom will not be able to get anything like full value from the expanded EU programme proposed. While more funding for preparatory language training is a possible short-term solution, it will not address the more strategic deep-seated British linguistic deficiency which requires long-term commitment and investment to sustain improvement.

401. While we welcome the Government's intention to give more emphasis to early language-training in schools it will clearly be many years, stretching beyond the termination of the proposed new EU programme, before that has any effect on the capacity of young British adults to take advantage of EU-funded education and training schemes. It is also likely to lead to a short-fall in the number of language teachers needed to provide early language-teaching in schools and, in our view, the reduction in compulsory language learning at secondary level will only make matters worse.

402. We therefore recommend that the Government should carry out an urgent reappraisal of language teaching policy, not only for the implications it will have for United Kingdom participation in the new EU programme but much more widely.

United Kingdom Business Engagement

403. We recommend that the Government should encourage the United Kingdom business sector to pay more attention to the new Programme and the opportunities it may offer for British business and to become more actively engaged in helping the Government to develop their strategy towards the Programme, especially for the *Leonardo* and *Grundtvig* programmes.

404. At local level, we recommend that the Government should encourage businesses to liaise with the Regional Development Agencies and sector skills councils, as well as with individual local education institutions, in developing projects under this programme that are relevant to British business needs and will be of benefit to individual businesses and their employees.

405. We also recommend that the Government take more active steps to promote the potential benefits of the programme, and especially the new *Leonardo* and *Grundtvig* programmes to British business, not only for the training and motivation of individual employees, but also more widely through the

corporate relationships and improved understanding of European processes and market opportunities which active involvement in these programmes should bring.

United Kingdom National Agency arrangements

406. We recommend that the present agency arrangements for administering the programmes in the United Kingdom should be retained, but that consideration should be given to forming a single over-arching advisory council, on the lines of the present separate United Kingdom Socrates-Erasmus and Leonardo Advisory Councils, designed so that interested bodies can contribute effectively to the formation of a comprehensive national strategy and review progress while leaving programme administration in the hands of the relevant agencies.

Final Recommendation

407. We commend this Report to the House and recommend that it should be debated by the House as soon as possible in the hope of drawing wider attention to the issues discussed in the Report and of influencing the European Commission and the Government in determining the final shape and details of the proposed programme.

APPENDIX 1: SUB-COMMITTEE G (SOCIAL AND CONSUMER AFFAIRS)

The Members of the Sub-Committee which conducted the Inquiry were:

      Lord Colwyn
      Earl of Dundee
      Baroness Greengross
      Baroness Howarth of Breckland
      Lord Harrison
      Lord Howie of Troon
      Baroness Massey of Darwen
      Lord Moser
      Baroness Neuberger
      Baroness Thomas of Walliswood (Chairman)
      Lord Trefgarne

Declaration of Interests:

Lord Colwyn
> *Practising Dental Surgeon*
> *President, All Party Group, Complementary and Integrated Healthcare*
> *President, National Medicines Society*
> *Chair, Campbell Montague International Ltd*
> *Chairman, Banbury Local Radio*

Earl of Dundee
> *No relevant Interests*

Baroness Greengross
> *Vice Chair, Britain in Europe*
> *President, Pensions Policy Institute*
> *Chief Executive, International Longevity Centre United Kingdom*
> *Chair, Experience Corps*
> *Board Member, HelpAge International*

Baroness Howarth of Breckland
> *Board Member, Food Standards Agency*
> *Board Member, CAFCASS (Children and Families Court Advisory and Support Service)*
> *Secretary, All Parliamentary Group for Children*
> *Patron and Trustee, Little Hearts Matter (health/care charity)*

Lord Harrison
> *No relevant Interests*

Lord Howie of Troon
> *No relevant Interests*

Baroness Massey of Darwen
> *Chair of the National Treatment Agency for Substance Misuse*
> *Co. Chair of APPG for Children*
> *School Governor*

Lord Moser
> *Board of Governors, LSE*
> *Board of Governors, Open Universities of Israel*
> *Board Member of National Research and Development Centre for Adult Literacy and Numeracy*

Baroness Neuberger

Member/Trustee of the British Council
Non-Executive Director, VHI (Irish health insurer)
Trustee, Imperial War Museum
Former Chancellor of Ulster University (1994-2000)
Advisor, Sainsbury Centre for Mental Health
Advisor, Jewish Community Centre for London

Baroness Thomas of Walliswood

No relevant Interests

Lord Trefgarne

Chairman, SEMTA
Director, United Kingdom Skills
President, IIE
President, METCOM

APPENDIX 2: CALL FOR EVIDENCE

The European Commission has published proposals for a Decision of the European Parliament and of the Council establishing an integrated action programme in the field of lifelong learning (*Commission Documents 11587/04 COM (2004) 474 final and 11587/04 ADD 1 SEC (2004) 971, 15 July 2004*).

These proposals aim to incorporate and build on the Commission's present education and training programmes and initiatives *(including Socrates, Leonardo da Vinci, Erasmus Mundus, the eLearning programme, Tempus and the Europass initiative)* by introducing a new comprehensive integrated life-long learning programme covering the period from 2007 to 2013. This will comprise the following specific programmes:

- Comenius for school-based education activities up to and including upper secondary level

- Erasmus for higher-level education and advanced training activities

- Leonardo da Vinci for all other aspects of vocational education and training, and,

- Grundtvig for adult education

A new **"transversal" programme** is also proposed for cross-cutting activities with specific emphasis on language and ICT-related learning activities which fall outside the specific programmes and for dissemination activities.

A new **Jean Monnet** programme would also be introduced from 2009 to support actions related to European integration and European education and training institutions and associations.

An indicative budget of €13.62 billion is proposed for the seven-year programme.

Sub-Committee G of the House of Lords EU Select Committee has decided to hold an Inquiry into these proposals with the aim of producing a Report to Parliament.

The Sub-Committee would be particularly interested in evidence from organisations and individuals with direct experience of current EU education and training programmes, and to learn whether those programmes were well-conceived and relevant, how well they worked in practice, whether they can be regarded as giving good value for money, what lessons might be learned from them and what use the United Kingdom has made of them.

As for the new programme, the Sub-Committee wishes to examine whether the proposals seem appropriate to the role of the Commission and relevant to the future needs of the EU, whether they appear to be clearly-defined and soundly-devised and whether they are likely to give good value for money, adding significantly to the education and training activities for which Member States have prime responsibility, as well as being simple and cost-effective to administer.

Interested parties are invited to submit written evidence to this Inquiry on any aspect of the Directive. Written evidence will need to be submitted to the House of Lords Committee Office by <u>Monday 10 January 2005.</u>

Evidence should be limited to four sides of A4 paper and should be set out in short numbered paragraphs. Supporting material, such as tables of figures or extracts from publications, may be attached to the submission, but should not exceed four extra pages. The submission should be signed and dated, together with a note of the author's name and status. It should make clear whether the evidence is submitted on an individual or corporate basis. Submissions by e-mail are preferred (as attachments in Word) with a signed hard copy to follow.

It would be helpful to have advance notice, by letter or e-mail, from those who are considering submitting written evidence.

Evidence submitted becomes the property of the Committee, and may be published. Witnesses may publicise their written evidence themselves, but in doing so should indicate that it was prepared for the Committee.

Having reviewed the written evidence, the Sub-Committee may decide to invite some of those who have submitted it to give oral evidence on the record to a public meeting of the Sub-Committee. Additional written information may also be requested.

APPENDIX 3: LIST OF WITNESSES

The following witnesses gave evidence. Those marked * gave oral evidence as well as written.

ALG European Service

ARCH*

Association of Colleges*

British Council*

Bristol University

Central Lancashire University

CILT, the National Centre for Languages

City & Guilds

Mark Cullens

Cumbria County Council Officers

Dr Paolo Dardanelli

Department for Education and Skills (DfES)*

ECOTEC

Educational Centres Association

European Commission*

Eurydice Unit at the National Foundation for Educational Research

Professor Robert Fisher

Glasgow University

Grampus Heritage & Training Ltd*

Lawrence Hardy

Help the Aged

HEURO

Marguerite Hogg*

Dr Kim Howells MP, Minister of State for Lifelong Learning, Further and Higher Education, DfES*

The IEE (Institution of Electrical Engineers)

Mr Ray Kirtley, University of Hull*

Ms Sue Laffey, Ounsdale High School, Staffordshire*

Learning and Skills Council*

Leeds University

Liverpool John Moores University

London Metropolitan University

Luton University

Sylvia Mingay*

Mr Martin Moorman, Ravenscliffe High School, Halifax*

Morthyng Ltd*

National Association of Language Advisers (NALA)

National Institute of Adult Continuing Education (NIACE)*

National Postgraduate Committee of the United Kingdom

North London Colleges European Network (NLCEN)

Open University

Plymouth College of Further Education

Ms Jill Ritchie, Bristol Local Education Authority*

SPRITO

Third Age Trust

David Tolliday, Projects Officer, Otley College

United Kingdom Erasmus Student Committee

United Kingdom Socrates-Erasmus Council*

Union of Industrial and Employers' Confederation of Europe (UNICE)

Universities Council for the Education of Teachers (UCET)

Universities United Kingdom (UUK)*

University Association for Contemporary European Studies (UACES)*

University Council of Modern Languages (UCML)

Professor Roger Vickerman

Welsh Assembly Government

Ms Julie Winyard, Benhall St Mary's CofE Primary School, Saxmundham*

Work Foundation

Workers' Educational Association (WEA)

APPENDIX 4: GLOSSARY

ABSSU	Adult Basic Skills Strategy Unit
A2	The second half of a full A-level qualification
ACL	Adult and community learning provision for adults previously funded by LEAs
ALI	Adult Learning Inspectorate
ALS	Additional learning support
APL	Accreditation of prior experience and learning
AS	Advanced Subsidiary: a stand-alone qualification valued as half a full A-level qualification
AVCE	Advanced Vocational Certificate of Education
CEDEFOP	European Centre for the Development of Vocational Training (an EU agency)
CoVE	Centre of Vocational Excellence
CPO	Community Punishment Order
CTC	Child Tax Credit
DDA	Disability Discrimination Act
DEL	Distributed and electronic learning
DELG	Distributed and Electronic Learning Group
DfES	Department for Education and Skills
DG	Directorate General
DL	Discretionary leave
E2E	Entry to employment
ECTS	European Credit Transfer System
EFL	English as a foreign language
ELE/R	Exceptional leave to enter or remain
EMA	Educational maintenance allowances, available nationally from 2004. (EMAs provide weekly payments to young people to encourage them to stay in education – to ensure that no 16-18-year-old is denied education because he or she cannot afford it.)
ERDF	European Regional Development Fund
ESF	European Social Fund, which supports projects targeting unemployment and workforce development
ESOL	English for speakers of other languages

ETPs	Employer Training Pilots, which encourage training in small firms by reimbursing smaller employers that release staff for training in normal working hours. Pilots launched in April 2002 were so successful that the Treasury committed £130 million to extend them.
FE	Further education
FEFC	Further Education Funding Council, now replaced by the Learning and Skills Council
FSMQ	Free-standing mathematics qualification
FTE	Full-time equivalent
glh	Guided learning hours
GNVQ	General National Vocational Qualification
GO	Government Office
HA	Housing association
HE	Higher education
HEFCE	Higher Education Funding Council for England
HEI	Higher Education Institution
HESA	Higher Education Statistics Agency
HNC	Higher National Certificate
HND	Higher National Diploma
HP	Humanitarian protection
IAG	The provision of precise information, advice and guidance to people about learning opportunities. The activity is crucial to ensure that learners enrol on the learning programme most suitable to their ability and aspirations.
IB	International Baccalaureate
ICT	Information and communications technology
IEE	Institute of Electrical Engineers
ILE/R	Indefinite leave to enter or remain
ILIAD	International Languages Inservice at a Distance
ILR	Individualised Learner Record – the data collection from LSC-funded providers. (This provides comprehensive data about learners and is returned regularly throughout the year. The ILR replaced the individualised student record (ISR) from 2002/03.)
IMD	Index of Multiple Deprivation

IT	Information technology
IVQs	International Vocational Qualifications
JANET	Joint Academic Network
JSA	Jobseekers' Allowance
LAD	Learning-aim database (at www.lscdata.gov.uk)
LEA	Local education authority
Learndirect	The brand name for provision delivered by learning centres and Ufi hubs (q.v.)
LIS	Learner Information Suite
Loadbands	Ranges of guided learning hours to which specific national base rates are allocated
LSDA	Learning and Skills Development Agency
LSC	Learning and Skills Council
MAN	Metropolitan Area Network
NASS	National Asylum Support Service
NLN	National Learning Network
NPS	National Probation Service
NQF	National Qualifications Framework
NRAG	National Rates Advisory Group – an independent group of provider representatives that advises the LSC on the national funding rates and programme weightings for all provision funded by the LSC
NTOs	National Training Organisations
NVQ	National Vocational Qualification
OCN	Open college network
Ofsted	Office for Standards in Education
OHCMI	Office of Her Majesty's Chief Inspector
OLSU	Offenders' Learning and Skills Unit (part of the DfES)
OSAT	Onsite Assessment and Training. About 1.5m people work in construction, but fewer than 20 per cent are qualified to the required NVQ standard. OSAT, jointly developed with the Construction Industry Training Board, is a fast-track solution.
OU	Open University
P4P	Partnerships for Progression – a joint initiative with the Higher Education Funding Council for England to increase participation in higher education (HE). The

Government's target is that, by 2010, 50 per cent of all 18–30-year-olds should have experienced higher education.

PFA	Provider Financial Assurance
QAA	Quality Assurance Agency for Higher Education
QCA	Qualifications and Curriculum Authority
RDA	Regional Development Agency
RSL	Registered social landlord
SRB	Single regeneration budget
SSC	Sector Skills Council
SMEs	Small and Medium Enterprises
StARS	Strategic Area Reviews, which began in April 2003. They review all the education and training (except for HE) that is on offer for 16-year-olds and above in each of the LSC local areas, identifying a true picture of the education and learning provision in an area of England and enabling recommendations for change.
Ufi	(Originally, "University for industry") Organisation with overall accountability and responsibility for hubs that contract with providers to deliver learndirect provision
UPIN	Unique provider identification number
VC SECTOR	Voluntary and Community Sector
VCE	Vocational Certificate of Education (vocational A-level)
WBL	Work-based learning for young people
WEA	Workers' Educational Association
WTC	Working Tax Credit

Printed in the United Kingdom by The Stationery Office Limited
4/2005   305389   19585

ISBN 0-10-400663-3